THE ACCIDENTAL
VEGAN

THE ACCIDENTAL
VEGAN

DEVRA GARTENSTEIN

CELESTIAL ARTS
Berkeley | Toronto

For Cintia

Celestial Arts
an imprint of Ten Speed Press
PO Box 7123
Berkeley, California 94707
www.tenspeed.com

Distributed in Australia by Simon and Schuster Australia, in Canada by Ten Speed
Press Canada, in New Zealand by Southern Publishers Group, in South Africa by
Real Books, and in the United Kingdom and Europe by Publishers Group UK.

Cover and text design by Tracy White
Food styling for bottom front cover photo by Kim Konecny
Prop styling for bottom front cover photo by Christine Wolheim

Previously published by Crossing Press, 2000.

Library of Congress Cataloging-in-Publication Data

Gartenstein, Devra.
    The accidental vegan / Devra Gartenstein.
    p. cm.
    "An update of a well-loved vegan cookbook filled with simple recipes that will
appeal to a wide range of health-minded home cooks"—Provided by publisher.
    Includes index.
    ISBN 978-1-58761-338-8
    1. Vegan cookery. 2. Cookery, International. I. Title.
    TX837.G322 2009
    641.5'636—dc22
                                                    2008033601

Printed in Canada on recycled paper (100% PCW)
First printing this edition, 2009

1 2 3 4 5 6 7 8 9 10 — 13 12 11 10 09

CONTENTS

PREFACE

I get mixed reactions to the title of this book. Some people say, "That's me!" Others seem offended at the suggestion that there could be anything accidental about choosing a vegan diet. I wasn't a vegan when I first wrote most of these recipes and I'm not a vegan now, although lately I've been avoiding most animal products in order to keep my cholesterol level down. I've read reviews holding that someone who isn't strictly vegan has no place writing a vegan cookbook. I disagree!

There are so many good reasons for us to collectively eat less meat and dairy. My personal health concerns have shown me firsthand that it makes sense to limit consumption of animal products. There are environmental and humanitarian reasons as well. A United Nations report early in 2007 fingered livestock as the single largest source of greenhouse gases, contributing more toward global warming than even transportation.

Rising food costs all over the globe can be traced in part to rising standards of living in formerly poor countries, increasing the demand for meat, which exacts a heavy toll on the planet's resources in comparison to plant-based foods. Too much land is being used to grow feed for livestock rather than food for humans, and as a result, there isn't enough food to go around.

My current business includes a farmers' market concession serving vegetarian dishes based on local, seasonal ingredients. Nearly every day I hear someone commenting, "Smells wonderful, but I'm not a vegetarian." I tell them that you don't have to be vegetarian or vegan to eat vegetarian or vegan food, just like you don't have to be Thai to eat Thai food, but they're not convinced. I want to find a way to reach these people, to encourage them not to automatically reject this cuisine just because it doesn't happen to have meat. I doubt that any of them includes meat in every single one of their meals, even those who proudly proclaim, "I'm a carnivore!" Toast and coffee is a vegetarian meal, and so are pancakes, waffles, and many mainstream soups.

I've come to believe that much of the resistance I encounter toward vegetarian and vegan food runs much deeper than the meal currently at hand. Meat has always been a special food for humans, from the times of Paleolithic hunters and ancient religious sacrifices to the modern-day Thanksgiving turkey tradition. It's no accident that the biblical tale recounts a divine preference for Abel's meat over Cain's vegetables (and it's equally telling that Cain, the farmer, is the survivor). These ancient stories speak of a bias or preference that is still largely with us, despite the fact that so much of the contemporary meat supply is mass-produced, diseased, and dirty.

Despite our long history of viewing meat as special, it really shouldn't be so hard to market meatless meals. Tasty food is tasty food, regardless of what's in it or not in it. Some of the resistance I encounter can no doubt be traced back to the bland, austere fodder that characterized the early natural foods movement, when health invariably trumped flavor and even salt, vinegar, and spices were suspect. Unfortunately, these stereotypes have persisted even as vegetarian and vegan food has come into its own as a vibrant cuisine during the past thirty years or so.

Another reason for the persistent negative image of the vegetarian and vegan movements may be the evangelical tone of so much of the outreach. The very terms *vegetarian* and *vegan* describe a diet completely free of meat products or animal products, respectively. Despite all of the excellent reasons to eat this way, only a small percentage of people have taken the step of completely renouncing these foods. Perhaps a piecemeal approach would be more effective, at least for some. After all, every meal that doesn't include meat lessens the demand for it and the toll it takes on our planet, regardless of whether or not the person eating it is a strict vegetarian or vegan.

The purpose of this book is not to convert anyone to a strictly vegan diet, although I'd certainly be happy to see more people eating this way. Instead, I'm hoping that more of us can learn to prepare a range of foods that are healthy and sustainable without necessarily thinking in those all-or-nothing terms, which can get in the way of taking smaller steps on a daily basis.

Many of the recipes in this book come from culinary traditions other than the Anglo-American style, which evolved in the context of a powerful cattle industry and wide-open spaces for grazing. The foods we find in other parts of the world tend to use meat sparingly because the real cost of producing animal products hasn't been obscured by an infrastructure geared toward producing these foods cheaply. The Western meat-based social and economic bias hides expenses such as environmental degradation, destruction of indigenous traditions, and rampant health problems. We have a great deal to learn from those societies that haven't had the luxury of this widespread denial.

Virtually every culture in the world has evolved a language of food as a way to create order and meaning out of its own unique ecological niche. The cuisine of a people expresses its values and its personality, its ingenuity and its quirks. As we grapple with the limitations of the Western cultural model, the foods and flavors of other regions can guide us in building a new relationship with our own landscape, one that helps the land regenerate and gives each of us some of the tools we need to restore our personal health.

The world of sustainable food and healthy eating sometimes feels like a vast minefield. No sooner do we learn that a certain food, such as fat, is bad for us than we start hearing that it may not be that harmful after all. Meat contains cholesterol and saturated fat, but grass-fed beef may have much less. Vegetarian and vegan eating can lessen the risk of heart disease and some cancers, but vegan diets can be deficient in vitamin B_{12}, an essential nutrient. Organic food is better for the environment, but less so when it's shipped from far away.

It can be especially difficult to make consistently good choices because we eat several times a day and there aren't always good options to be found wherever we happen to find ourselves when we're hungry. To make matters worse, the advertising industry latches onto each new study, and huge food conglomerates are quick to introduce products that exploit the kernel of truth in every fresh discovery. It's enough to make anyone feel cynical or discouraged.

I think about food day in and day out, but I try not to set impossibly high standards for myself because the issues are so complex and the choices so numerous. I'm wary of absolutes and simple answers when it comes to everything from vegetarianism and veganism to organics and eating locally to industrial agriculture and processed foods. Eating well is an ongoing quest, and I want to approach it with an open mind and a sense of humor.

If you want to take part in this dialog further—whether you agree or disagree with my ruminations—you can visit my blog at quirkygourmet.com and leave comments. I write about these issues regularly, and I look forward to feedback. In the meantime, please go ahead and enjoy the food!

INTRODUCTION

Cooking starts with shopping: deciding where to go for our raw materials. That's a choice that takes into account everything from what's closest to what we can afford to what matters to us in the larger scheme of things, like our feelings about compassion or the environment. I've heard people say that they'd like to eat more vegetarian food but they can't afford it. That always strikes me as strange, as vegetables are usually less expensive than meat, at least when they're of like quality. But there really isn't any vegetarian equivalent of McDonald's or Taco Bell, with ninety-nine cent meals and cheap, supersized portions.

The fact is, we spend money on what matters to us. I know people who are barely scraping by who buy almost all of their food at farmers' markets, and I've met people who live in mansions who fill their cupboards with processed garbage from big-box warehouses. I try for a middle ground. I will sometimes buy mainstream products that aren't grown organically, but I do look for items that have no preservatives or other artificial ingredients.

It's great to buy organic foods, but it can be difficult to know whether a producer is just hopping on the bandwagon and making money from the latest trend or carefully creating a clean product because they believe in healthful food. It's easier to tell the difference when we can meet producers face to face, like at a farmers' market or a neighborhood bakery.

EATING WELL WHILE SPENDING LESS

Although good food costs more than processed food, you don't necessarily have to spend a lot of money to eat well. Sure, some quality items are costly, like fine olive oil and organic produce, but there are also plenty of wonderful foods that are very affordable, even in an age of rapidly climbing prices. I try to look for a happy medium, like picking a decent olive oil that isn't terribly expensive, or choosing organics when the price isn't that much higher than conventional produce.

Above all, it's important to know what different foods usually cost and to be aware of the price of each item you put in your shopping cart. Don't automatically buy the cheapest thing, but don't spend more than you have to just because you're not paying attention. Try not to assume that something is better just because it's more expensive. Get to know your own preferences and priorities so you can make solid, conscious decisions about when it's worthwhile to pay more. Note the price per pound when you're buying bulk items, and be aware of how many pounds you're putting in the bag.

If you enjoy shopping and you have the time for it, get to know the ethnic specialty stores and corner produce stands in your area. Items like rice noodles and dried chiles are often quite a bit cheaper in shops that specialize in these types of food. Neighborhood fruit and vegetable stands tend to have great prices on fresh offerings. Many of them also have their own particular specialties. There's one place I frequent that consistently has cheap, perfectly ripe avocados, and another one with great prices on fresh herbs.

Eat fruits and vegetables in season. Artichokes, asparagus, and snow peas can be three or four times as expensive in the winter as they are in the spring. Unlike cars or furniture, with produce low prices often correlate with high quality. Fruits and vegetables in season are abundant and fresh, while out of season they tend to be wilted and jet-lagged, or tasteless because they've been harvested prematurely.

Don't assume that you're getting a great price on everything you buy in a big-box discount store. Items at these mega warehouses can certainly be cheaper, but I also see plenty of items there that I can buy cheaper someplace else, and in smaller quantities. Keep in mind that if you buy more than you need in order to get a lower unit price, you're not really saving any money.

While we all want to save money on groceries, there are also times when it makes sense to spend more. According to Eric Schlosser, author of *Fast Food Nation*, Americans today spend a smaller percentage of our income on food than any other culture in the history of the world. I've heard figures ranging from 11 to 15 percent. Whatever the exact number, it's partly a result of federal policies aimed at preventing the kind of widespread discontent that occurred when food prices rose during the 1970s, causing angry housewives to boycott meat and picket grocery stores.

To keep food prices low, the government now pays subsidies to farmers for growing staple crops, especially corn and soy. As a result of these payments, we're so overloaded with these foods that ranchers feed them to livestock and chemists devise new ways to use them. Their experiments have yielded, among other things, the sweetener high-fructose corn syrup, which is now used in most soft drinks, as well as many processed foods. Some researchers have linked the rising incidence of adult-onset diabetes to the introduction of this highly processed corn syrup into our diets.

It's quite possible that we'd spend less on health care if we opted for better, more wholesome foods. But it still makes sense to pay attention to prices and make informed purchasing decisions.

ORGANICS

Organic foods are produced without chemical fertilizers and pesticides. Of course that's something we all want. After all, cleaner food means healthier bodies and a less toxic planet. But organics have become big business during the past twenty years. As the organic movement has grown increasingly popular and mainstream, it's become something of a mixed blessing.

Until relatively recently, few states had any kind of system in place for regulating organic products. Anyone could claim their products were organic, whether or not they actually were. This became a real problem as consumers showed that they were willing to pay more for food that was produced without chemicals. As a result, the organic movement, which had started with a bunch of idealistic farmers and visionary entrepreneurs, soon spread to much larger corporations, who didn't necessarily share those values.

During the 1990s, Congress started moving toward regulations specifying how foods and other goods must be produced to be labeled as organic. They appointed a task force made up of industry lobbyists as well as forward-thinking farmers, who eventually came up with a list of standards that the big companies thought were too rigid but the little guys felt weren't strict enough.

In 2002, the National Organic Program was enacted. This legislation paved the way for all kinds of organic products that had little to do with the ideals that fueled the movement in its early days, like organic sugared breakfast cereals and highly processed organic cookies. "Industrial organic" farms now cultivate vast fields of individual crop varieties, using practices that look an awful lot like mainstream agriculture, minus the chemicals.

At the same time, the national organic certification standards spurred many people who were deeply concerned about wholesome food and sustainable farming to innovate and find new ways to set their offerings apart. Many small-scale producers who use organic methods are opting out of the costly and time-consuming certification process, choosing instead to market their products directly to consumers through community supported agriculture (CSA) programs, or by selling at farmers' markets.

Savvy consumers are looking for opportunities to buy products that are locally grown and produced, shortening the supply chain and lessening the amount of energy that goes into shipping and storage. There are many other benefits to this approach. Farmers who sell their crops locally tend to operate on a smaller scale than industrial farms. Even when they're not strictly organic, small-scale operations generally use fewer pesticides per acre than larger outfits. They're also more likely to intersperse rows of different crops, a practice that in itself lessens the need for pesticides.

So how do you decide what to buy? I recommend asking yourself what's most important to you. If you're looking to lessen the environmental impact of your personal food chain, it's as important to buy food that's produced locally as it is to buy organic food. If you're mainly concerned about health effects, you might want to choose all organic foods, regardless of where they're grown. And if you're especially interested in building community, choose items that are locally produced. No matter which of these issues is your greatest priority, if you support your local farmers' market you'll find foods that fit all of these criteria.

APPETIZERS

HUMMUS

MAKES ABOUT 2 1/2 CUPS

Hummus, one of the world's great dips, goes well with raw veggies, crackers, tortilla chips, or pita bread. If you use more olive oil, you'll make a richer hummus; if you use less, you'll make one that's lower in fat.

1 clove garlic

1 to 2 tablespoons extra-virgin olive oil

2 cups cooked chickpeas, or 1 (15-ounce) can, drained and rinsed

1 tablespoon chopped parsley

3 tablespoons freshly squeezed lemon juice

$\frac{1}{4}$ cup tahini

1 teaspoon sea salt

$\frac{1}{2}$ cup water

Combine the garlic and oil in a food processor and pulse until the garlic is finely chopped. Add the chickpeas, parsley, lemon juice, tahini, and salt, and process briefly. With the machine running, slowly add the water and process until smooth.

ANASAZI BEAN DIP

MAKES 3 CUPS

Although pinto beans are commonly used in bean dips, Anasazi beans, with their fuller flavor, are a nice change of pace. You can find them in natural food stores and specialty markets. You need to soak the beans for at least a few hours before cooking, so plan ahead.

2 cups dry Anasazi beans

4 cups water, or more as needed

1 onion, chopped

2 cloves garlic, minced

1 tomato, chopped, or 1 cup canned crushed tomatoes or tomato puree

1 (4-ounce) can diced mild green chiles, or 2 Anaheim chiles, diced

1 tablespoon chili powder, mild or hot

1 teaspoon ground cumin

1 teaspoon dried oregano

1 teaspoon sea salt

2 tablespoons red wine vinegar

Cover the beans in water about 1 inch deep over the beans and let soak for a few hours or overnight.

Drain and rinse the beans, put them in a large saucepan, and add the 4 cups water. Bring to a boil over high heat, then turn the heat down to medium-low, cover, and simmer for 30 minutes. Stir in the onion, garlic, tomato, chiles, chili powder, cumin, oregano, and salt. Continue cooking for about 1 hour, until the beans are soft enough to break down when you stir them. Add more water if needed to prevent sticking. At the end of the cooking time, the beans should be thick and saucy.

When the beans are fully cooked, stir in the vinegar and serve the dip hot or cold, with veggies or chips.

FUL MADAMAS (FAVA BEAN DIP)

MAKES 2 CUPS

A cousin of Hummus (page 2) and Baba Ghanoush (page 6), Ful Madamas goes quite well with both of them. Egyptians serve the three dips together in separate mounds on a large plate and call the arrangement *mezze*.

1 tablespoon olive oil

2 cloves garlic, minced

1 tablespoon chopped parsley

1 (14-ounce) can fava beans, drained

1 tablespoon freshly squeezed lemon juice

1 teaspoon dried spearmint

1/2 teaspoon sea salt

Freshly ground black pepper

Heat the oil in a small skillet over medium-low heat, add the garlic and parsley, and sauté for 1 minute. Stir in the beans, lemon juice, spearmint, and salt. Season to taste with pepper and cook until heated through, stirring and mashing the beans a bit as they cook. Serve warm or at room temperature.

VEGGIE-WALNUT PÂTÉ

MAKES 2 TO 3 CUPS

This recipe is vaguely reminiscent of chopped liver (in the best possible way, if you can imagine that!). Serve it on crackers. If you want to add an extra layer of flavor, you can roast the walnuts (see Pantry, page 211).

$1/2$ cup walnuts

2 cups of a combination of any of the following veggies, coarsely chopped: carrots, green beans, zucchini, broccoli, cauliflower, cooked winter squash, or red and green bell peppers

8 to 10 mushrooms

2 shallots, chopped

1 clove garlic, minced

2 tablespoons olive oil

1 teaspoon dried basil

1 teaspoon dried marjoram

Sea salt

Freshly ground black pepper

1 tablespoon freshly squeezed lemon juice

Chop the walnuts, mixed veggies, mushrooms, shallots, and garlic in a food processor until they're the consistency of coarse bread crumbs. If your food processor is small, chop them in batches.

Heat the oil in a small saucepan over medium-low heat and sauté the veggie mixture, basil, and marjoram for 6 to 8 minutes, until they start to brown. Season with salt and pepper to taste, stir in the lemon juice, and serve warm or cold.

BABA GHANOUSH

MAKES 2 CUPS

Serve this dip with Hummus (page 2) and pita bread for a light and satisfying meal.

2 eggplants

¼ cup tahini

2 tablespoons freshly squeezed lemon juice

1 tablespoon extra-virgin olive oil

2 cloves garlic, minced

1 tablespoon chopped parsley, or 1 teaspoon dried

1 teaspoon sea salt

½ teaspoon freshly ground black pepper

Preheat the oven to 400°F.

Poke the eggplants all over with a fork or knife, then bake on a cookie sheet until they're wrinkled and soft, about 1 hour.

When the eggplants are cool enough to handle, scoop out the pulp and transfer to a food processor or blender. Add the tahini, lemon juice, olive oil, garlic, parsley, salt, and pepper and process until smooth. Serve at room temperature.

AFGHANI EGGPLANT DIP

MAKES 2 CUPS

Afghanistan lies between the Middle East and India, and as a result, it has a wonderful crossroads cuisine that brings together two fine sets of flavors.

2 eggplants

2 tablespoons freshly squeezed lemon juice

2 cloves garlic, minced

1 tablespoon chopped parsley

1 tablespoon chopped mint

$\frac{1}{2}$ teaspoon dried dill

$\frac{1}{2}$ teaspoon ground cumin

$\frac{1}{4}$ teaspoon ground cardamom

1 teaspoon sea salt

Preheat the oven to 400°F.

Poke the eggplants all over with a fork or knife, then bake on a cookie sheet until they're wrinkled and soft, about 1 hour.

When the eggplants are cool enough to handle, scoop out the pulp and transfer to a food processor or blender. Add the lemon juice, garlic, parsley, mint, dill, cumin, cardamom, and salt, and process until smooth. Serve at room temperature.

ARTICHOKE DIP

MAKES 2 CUPS

This dip is so flavorful that it's hard to believe it doesn't harden your arteries! It's a great alternative to typical recipes for artichoke dip, which usually contain tons of mayonnaise and cream cheese.

1 (14-ounce) can artichoke hearts, drained

8 ounces soft tofu

2 tablespoons chopped basil

1 tablespoon freshly squeezed lemon juice

1 tablespoon extra-virgin olive oil

Sea salt

Combine the artichoke hearts, tofu, basil, lemon juice, and olive oil in a food processor or blender and process until smooth and creamy. Season with salt to taste and serve at room temperature or chilled.

ROASTED PEPPER DIP

I once made this dip for a party I catered, and one enthusiastic woman kept exclaiming, "It's like life! This dip tastes like life!"

1 (8-ounce) jar roasted red bell peppers, drained

1 (14-ounce) can artichoke hearts, drained

1/2 cup whole almonds

1 clove garlic, minced

1 tablespoon freshly squeezed lemon juice

1/2 cup tightly packed basil leaves

Combine all of the ingredients in a food processor or blender and process until smooth. Serve at room temperature or chilled.

EGG ROLLS

MAKES 15 TO 20 EGG ROLLS

These egg rolls can be an appetizer or a meal in themselves. They taste a lot like the traditional Chinese version, minus the pork or shrimp. Serve them with Plum Sauce (page 29), Teriyaki Marinade (page 34), and Chinese hot mustard on the side. When purchasing the wrappers, check the ingredients list to be sure they don't contain eggs. For tips on deep–frying, see Basic Techniques, page 219.

1 tablespoon olive oil

1 onion, chopped

1 clove garlic, minced

1 tablespoon grated ginger

1 carrot, grated

6 to 8 mushrooms, minced

1 cup finely chopped bok choy or napa cabbage

½ cup bean sprouts

1 (5-ounce) can water chestnuts, drained and finely chopped

1 (5-ounce) can bamboo shoots in strips, drained

2 tablespoons soy sauce, or more to taste

1 teaspoon toasted sesame oil

1 (12-ounce) package egg roll or spring roll wrappers

Corn, peanut, or vegetable oil for frying

Heat the olive oil in a saucepan over medium-low heat, add the onion, garlic, and ginger, and sauté for about 5 minutes, until the onion is soft. Stir in the carrot, mushrooms, bok choy, sprouts, water chestnuts, bamboo shoots, soy sauce, and sesame oil and cook, stirring occasionally, for another 10 minutes, until the vegetables are soft.

To assemble the rolls, lay a wrapper in front of you diagonally, like a diamond. Spoon 2 to 3 tablespoons of filling, with as little juice as possible, in a horizontal line across the middle. Fold the bottom corner toward the middle, then fold the side corners over toward the center. With your finger, spread a bead of water along the remaining edges—the flap of the envelope—then roll the egg roll up from bottom to top as tightly as you can without ripping the wrapper. The wet edges should seal the roll.

Heat 1 inch of corn oil to about 360°F in a large skillet over medium-high heat. Carefully lower a few rolls at a time into the skillet and cook for about 3 minutes, then gently turn and continue cooking for about 3 minutes longer, until they're brown on both sides.

Transfer to paper towels or clean brown bags to drain, and continue frying the rest of the egg rolls.

POT STICKERS

MAKES ABOUT 40 POT STICKERS

There's something so satisfying about a savory mixture wrapped in dough. Think of tortellini, ravioli, pierogi, or kreplach. When purchasing the wrappers, check the ingredients list and make sure they don't contain eggs.

1 tablespoon olive oil

1 onion, finely chopped

1 clove garlic, minced

1 tablespoon grated ginger

1 carrot, grated

6 to 8 mushrooms, minced

1 cup finely chopped bok choy or napa cabbage

1/2 cup bean sprouts

1 (5-ounce) can water chestnuts, drained and finely chopped

1 (5-ounce) can bamboo shoots, drained and finely chopped

2 tablespoons soy sauce, or more to taste

1 teaspoon toasted sesame oil

1 (10-ounce) package wonton or pot sticker wrappers

1 tablespoon peanut or canola oil

1/2 cup water

Heat the olive oil in a saucepan over medium-low heat, add the onion, garlic, and ginger, and sauté for about 5 minutes, until the onion is soft. Add the carrot, mushrooms, bok choy, sprouts, water chestnuts, bamboo shoots, soy sauce, and sesame oil and sauté for another 10 minutes, until the vegetables are tender.

To assemble the pot stickers, put a small teaspoonful of filling in the center of each wrapper. With your finger, spread a bead of water along the edges of the top half of the wrapper, then fold the wrapper up over the filling and press the edges together.

Heat the peanut oil in a large skillet and pan-fry the pot stickers for about 1 minute. Add the water, cover the pan, and cook for 6 to 8 minutes longer. Serve hot or warm.

HUMMUS AND ROASTED PEPPER ROLL-UPS

MAKES ABOUT 36 BITE-SIZED PIECES

These bite-sized spirals are quick and easy to assemble. That's a good thing, as they disappear quickly, so you may need to make more!

6 (10-inch) flour tortillas

2 cups Hummus (page 2)

1 (8-ounce) jar roasted red bell peppers, drained and cut into thin strips

With a spatula, cover a tortilla with a thin layer of hummus. Arrange a small handful of pepper strips in a thin line, starting at the top of the tortilla and ending at the bottom.

Roll the tortilla from left to right as tightly as you can without squeezing out the hummus and peppers, then slice the roll in bite-sized pieces. Discard (or eat) the end pieces.

Repeat with the remaining ingredients.

MU SHU VEGGIE ROLLS

When you order a mu shu plate in a Chinese restaurant, you get a variety of components that you assemble into burrito-like rolls. In this recipe you assemble them ahead of time to serve as appetizers.

8 ounces firm tofu, cut in strips

1 cup Plum Sauce (page 29)

1 tablespoon olive oil

$\frac{1}{2}$ onion, minced

2 cloves garlic, minced

1 tablespoon grated ginger

3 carrots, grated

1 bunch baby bok choy (about 1 pound), chopped

1 tablespoon soy sauce

8 to 10 (8-inch) flour tortillas

1 cup cooked brown rice

Marinate the tofu in half of the plum sauce for at least 10 minutes.

Heat the oil in a saucepan over medium-low heat, add the onion, garlic, and ginger, and sauté for 5 minutes, until the onion is soft. Add the carrots, bok choy, and soy sauce and sauté for another 5 minutes, until the vegetables are tender. Turn off the heat and add the marinated tofu along with 2 tablespoons of its marinade.

Spread a layer of remaining plum sauce in a line down the middle of each tortilla, then layer a heaping tablespoon of rice and $\frac{1}{2}$ cup of the veggie mixture over the plum sauce. Roll up like a burrito, then repeat with the remaining ingredients, and serve.

SPRING ROLLS

Serve these refreshing, crunchy appetizers with Peanut Sauce (page 32).

8 ounces thin rice noodles

20 leaves basil, coarsely chopped

20 leaves mint, coarsely chopped

2 cups baby salad greens

8 ounces firm tofu, cut in long, thin strips

1 tablespoon grated ginger

1/4 cup soy sauce

2 tablespoons freshly squeezed lime juice

1 (16-ounce) package rice paper spring roll wrappers

Put the noodles in a bowl, pour in boiling water to cover by a couple of inches, and soak the noodles for 10 minutes, until soft. Drain the noodles, rinse with cold water, and shake the colander to get rid of any excess moisture. Return the noodles to the bowl, add the basil, mint, salad greens, tofu, ginger, soy sauce, and lime juice, and mix well.

Prepare a bowl of warm water large enough to dip the spring roll wrappers. Briefly dip 6 wrappers, one at a time, into the warm water, then spread them on a work surface in front of you. Put 1/4 cup filling on each wrapper. The wrappers should soften by the time you get the filling onto all of them.

Fold the bottom of the first wrapper up over the filling, then fold each side toward the center. Roll from the bottom to the top of each roll as tightly as you can without ripping the rice paper. If you do rip it, just roll another wrapper around the whole thing when you do the next batch. Repeat this process with the remaining ingredients.

NORI ROLLS

Slices of this crunchy, flavorful vegetarian sushi make a colorful appetizer tray. You'll need a bamboo sushi mat, which you can buy in natural food stores and Asian groceries. While you're there, also look for the umeboshi plum paste, wasabi, pickled ginger, and nori, a seaweed product pressed into rectangular sheets. You can buy nori toasted, in which case you can use it right out of the package. Otherwise, toast it for a few seconds by holding it about a foot over a low flame on a stovetop burner or over an electric burner set on low heat. The nori will turn dark green when it's ready.

4 cups water

2 cups short-grain brown rice

2 tablespoons grated ginger

3 tablespoons rice vinegar

3 tablespoons tahini

3 tablespoons soy sauce, plus more for serving

10 sheets toasted nori

4 carrots, cut into sticks 3 to 5 inches long

20 green beans, trimmed

5 teaspoons umeboshi paste

Wasabi paste, for serving

Pickled ginger, for serving

Bring the water to a boil in a saucepan over high heat, then stir in the rice, lower the heat, cover, and simmer for about 45 minutes, until all of the water is absorbed. Meanwhile, soak the ginger in the rice vinegar for at least 15 minutes.

When the rice is ready, transfer it to a large bowl, add the tahini, soy sauce, and the ginger mixture, and stir until thoroughly combined. Spread it in a thin layer against the bowl, then put it in the refrigerator to cool.

When the rice is mostly cool, lay a sheet of nori on the sushi mat with the long side facing you (the strips of bamboo in the sushi mat should also be oriented horizontally).

Spread about $1/2$ cup of the rice mixture across the lower third of the nori, starting about 1 inch from the edge of the nori closest to you. Arrange 2 carrot sticks and 2 green beans in a horizontal line along the center of the rice. Roll the mat tightly around the nori, using the mat to press the roll together. Spread about $1/2$ teaspoon of umeboshi paste along the upper edge of the nori, then finish rolling and gently press on the seam to seal. Repeat with the remaining ingredients.

Cut each roll into 6 to 8 pieces. This will be easiest if you use a sharp or a serrated knife.

Serve with soy sauce, wasabi, and pickled ginger.

DOLMADES

Dolmades, or stuffed grape leaves, are a common food in the Middle East. This Greek version is delicious with Tahini Dressing (page 48) served alongside. If you have access to fresh grape leaves, you can brine them yourself. Pick them in late spring, when they're about the size of a woman's hand. Boil them in salted water for 10 to 15 minutes, until they soften.

2 tablespoons olive oil

1 onion, minced

2 cups cooked short-grain brown rice

2 tablespoons tomato paste

1/2 cup raw sunflower seeds

1/2 teaspoon ground cinnamon

2 tablespoons freshly squeezed lemon juice

1/2 teaspoon sea salt

Pinch of freshly ground black pepper

1 (8-ounce) jar grape leaves, drained

Heat 1 tablespoon of the oil in a small saucepan over medium-low heat, add the onion, and sauté for about 5 minutes, until soft. Stir in the rice, tomato paste, sunflower seeds, cinnamon, lemon juice, salt, and pepper and remove from the heat.

Preheat the oven to 375°F. Oil an 8-inch square baking pan.

Spread 10 grape leaves on a work surface with the darker side facing down. Spoon a heaping tablespoon of filling onto each leaf. Fold the bottom up over the filling, fold the sides toward the middle, and then roll toward the top. Arrange the rolled leaves closely together in the prepared pan, seam side down, and brush the tops with the remaining tablespoon of oil. Cover with foil and bake for 35 to 40 minutes, until the leaves are tender. Serve hot or cold.

STUFFED MUSHROOMS

MAKES 10 TO 15 STUFFED MUSHROOMS

My mother makes these appetizers on special occasions, using butter rather than olive oil. This vegan variation is close runner-up to her tasty version. Use the largest button mushrooms you can find, and peel them. You may wonder how to peel mushrooms. Here's how you do it: When you remove the stem from a large mushroom, the skin in the middle will start to separate from the head. Use this as your starting point to peel away the rest of the skin. This makes the mushrooms especially tender.

1 pound large mushrooms

4 tablespoons olive oil

1 onion, chopped

1 teaspoon sea salt

1 teaspoon dried basil

1 cup bread crumbs

Preheat the oven to 375°F.

Remove the stems from the mushrooms and, preferably, peel the caps (see headnote). Finely chop the stems.

Heat 2 tablespoons of the oil in a small skillet, add the mushroom stems and onion, and sauté for about 10 minutes, until the mushroom stems begin to release their moisture. Stir in the salt, basil, and bread crumbs.

Put about a tablespoon of filling in each mushroom, rounding the top with the spoon. Pour the remaining 2 tablespoons oil in an 8-inch square baking pan, set the mushrooms carefully in the pan, and bake for 45 to 55 minutes, until the tops start to brown.

DEEP-FRIED ARTICHOKE HEARTS

MAKES 15 TO 20 PIECES

Okay, this appetizer is indulgent, but once or twice a year maybe? Serve it with Basil Mayonnaise (page 36). Yum!

Corn or vegetable oil, for frying

1/2 cup unbleached white or whole wheat flour

1/2 teaspoon sea salt

1 (14-ounce) can quartered artichoke hearts, drained

Heat 1 inch of oil in a small skillet over medium-low heat for deep-frying (see Basic Techniques, page 217 for tips on deep-frying). Meanwhile, mix the flour and salt in a small bowl. Add the artichoke hearts and toss to evenly coat with the flour.

When the oil is hot (about 360°F), use tongs or a slotted spoon to add the artichoke hearts to the oil one at a time, waiting a few seconds after you add each one. Fry for 2 to 3 minutes, then turn them and fry for another 2 to 3 minutes, until they're brown on both sides. Transfer to paper towels or clean brown bags to drain. Serve warm or hot.

RICE BALLS WITH UMEBOSHI PLUMS

MAKES 6 BALLS

These rice balls are tasty and filling, with a tart and salty surprise at the center. They keep well and make an excellent snack to take along on a hike or bicycle ride. Watch for pits when you eat them! You can find black sesame seeds and umeboshi plums in Asian markets, as well as many natural food stores.

2 cups water

1 cup short-grain brown rice

1 tablespoon tahini

2 tablespoons soy sauce

1 tablespoon rice vinegar

1 teaspoon grated ginger

6 umeboshi plums

¼ cup black sesame seeds

Bring the water to a boil, then stir in the rice, lower the heat, cover, and simmer for 45 minutes, until all of the water is absorbed.

Let the rice stand until it's cool enough to handle, then mix it with the tahini, soy sauce, vinegar, and ginger. Shape the rice into balls with a 2½-inch diameter, wetting your hands if the rice sticks to them. Press a plum into the center of each ball and close the rice around it, then roll the balls in the sesame seeds. Serve warm or cold.

TOMATO-HERB BREAD

MAKES 6 SERVINGS

This appetizer is reminiscent of crostini, but easier to make. With the combination of basil, olives, and sun-dried tomatoes in fresh, warm bread, it's a nice accompaniment to pasta.

$\frac{1}{2}$ cup sun-dried tomatoes

1 cup tightly packed basil leaves

12 to 15 pitted kalamata olives

2 tablespoons olive oil

$\frac{1}{2}$ teaspoon sea salt

$\frac{1}{4}$ teaspoon freshly ground black pepper

1 loaf of wonderful crusty bread

Preheat the oven to 350°F. Soak the sun-dried tomatoes in boiling water for a few minutes, until softened.

Drain the tomatoes, then put them in a food processor or blender along with the basil, olives, oil, salt, and pepper. Process until almost smooth, stopping to scrape down the sides a few times if need be.

Slice the bread open lengthwise but not all the way through, and spread it with the tomato mixture. Close the bread back up, wrap it in foil, and bake for 10 minutes, until it's warm in the center. Slice the bread about 1 inch thick, open the slices, and arrange the pieces on a serving plate, with the cut side up.

SAUCES, MARINADES, AND CONDIMENTS

TOMATO SAUCE

MAKES ABOUT 4 CUPS

This is a classic and versatile tomato sauce. You can substitute fresh tomatoes and basil in this recipe. Add the tomatoes once the onions are soft, and the basil just a few minutes before the sauce is ready. Aside from its classic function as a pasta sauce, you can serve it over steamed veggies or as a topping for Polenta with Fresh Herbs (page 183) or Polenta with Olives and Sun-Dried Tomatoes (page 185).

1 tablespoon olive oil

1 onion, chopped

3 cloves garlic, minced

2 tablespoons dried basil

1 teaspoon dried oregano

1 teaspoon sea salt

$1/2$ teaspoon freshly ground black pepper

1 (28-ounce) can crushed tomatoes

Heat the oil in a saucepan over medium-low heat, add the onion, garlic, basil, oregano, salt, and pepper, and sauté for 5 minutes, until the onion is translucent.

Stir in the crushed tomatoes, lower the heat, cover, and simmer for at least 30 minutes, stirring regularly. Serve hot.

CASHEW-GINGER SAUCE

MAKES 2 TO 3 CUPS

This sauce is adapted from a Brazilian dish that traditionally has shrimp in it. I enjoy it served over steamed veggies. This recipe makes enough sauce for about 2 to 3 pounds of steamed veggies.

1 cup roasted cashews

1 tablespoon olive oil

1 onion, chopped

1 tablespoon grated ginger

1 cup canned crushed tomatoes or tomato puree

$1/2$ cup coconut milk

2 tablespoons chopped cilantro

1 teaspoon paprika

$1/2$ teaspoon sea salt

Put the cashews in a food processor and process until they have the consistency of cornmeal.

Heat the oil in a small saucepan over medium-low heat, add the onion and ginger, and sauté for about 5 minutes, until the onion is soft. Stir in the cashews, tomatoes, coconut milk, cilantro, paprika, and salt, and cook, stirring occasionally, for another 5 minutes, until heated through. Taste and add more salt if you like. Serve hot.

ROMESCO SAUCE

MAKES ABOUT 2 CUPS

Like its music and its architecture, the food of Spain is passionate. This tomato sauce, with its interplay of flavors and textures, is a perfect example. This is a nice sauce for steamed veggies. You can also use it as a dipping sauce with a fine loaf of crusty bread.

12 to 15 raw hazelnuts, with skins

6 to 8 pitted green olives

4 tomatoes, quartered

2 cloves garlic, finely minced

10 sprigs parsley

2 tablespoons red wine vinegar

1 teaspoon sea salt

$1/2$ teaspoon freshly ground black pepper

Put the hazelnuts and olives in a food processor or blender and pulse until coarsely chopped. Remove them and set them aside.

Put the tomatoes, garlic, parsley, vinegar, salt, and pepper in the food processor or blender and puree until smooth. Stir the hazelnuts and olives into the tomato puree and serve at room temperature.

PESTO

Pesto freezes well, so make plenty when basil is in season, then freeze it and enjoy it as long as your supply lasts. It's great on pasta or pizza. This version is much lower in fat than traditional recipes because it uses no cheese. It also breaks with tradition a bit by including sun-dried tomatoes, which gives it a deep, rich flavor.

$1/2$ cup sun-dried tomatoes

2 cloves garlic

3 cups loosely packed basil leaves

1 cup raw walnuts

2 tablespoons extra-virgin olive oil

$1/2$ cup chopped parsley

1 teaspoon sea salt

$1/2$ teaspoon freshly ground black pepper

Soak the sun-dried tomatoes in boiling water for a few minutes, until softened.

Put the garlic in a food processor or blender and pulse a few times to chop finely. Drain the sun-dried tomatoes and add to the garlic, along with the basil, walnuts, olive oil, parsley, salt, and pepper. Process until smooth. If you mix it with pasta or veggies that have just been cooked, don't reheat the mixture further, as you'll risk burning it. You can also serve pesto cold, as a spread on bread or crackers.

MUFFULETTA SAUCE

MAKES 1 1/2 CUPS

Muffuletta is a type of sandwich that originated in New Orleans, which makes use of a piquant olive salad spread on bread. That olive salad was the inspiration for this sauce, which you can also use as a warmed sauce for steamed veggies or as a cold dip for raw veggies.

8 to 10 sun-dried tomatoes

1 clove garlic

1 (14-ounce) can artichoke hearts, drained

8 to 10 pitted kalamata olives

1/4 cup basil leaves, tightly packed

1 tablespoon extra-virgin olive oil

1 teaspoon sea salt

Freshly ground black pepper

Soak the sun-dried tomatoes in boiling water for a few minutes, until softened.

Put the garlic in a food processor or blender and pulse a few times to chop the garlic. Drain the sun-dried tomatoes and add to the garlic, along with the artichoke hearts, olives, basil, olive oil, and salt. Process until smooth, then season to taste with pepper.

FENNEL TAPENADE

This tapenade is so flavorful that a little bit goes a long way. A couple of kids I know insist they hate olives, but you can't keep them away from this sauce!

1 small bulb fennel, cored and chopped

½ cup pitted kalamata olives

2 tablespoons chopped red onion

1 small clove garlic, minced

2 tablespoons extra-virgin olive oil

1 tablespoon red wine vinegar

Combine all of the ingredients in a food processor or blender and process until smooth. Serve hot with pasta, or cold as a spread on bread or crackers.

PLUM SAUCE

Use this sweet and salty sauce for egg rolls or pot stickers, or as a marinade for tofu, as in the Mu Shu Veggie Rolls (page 14).

2 (4-ounce) jars plum baby food

2 tablespoons soy sauce

1 teaspoon toasted sesame oil

Whisk all of the ingredients together. Serve at room temperature.

SESAME SAUCE

MAKES 3 CUPS

I developed this recipe while trying to duplicate the cold sesame noodles from my favorite Chinese restaurant. Toss it with Asian noodles or spaghetti, and serve it topped with chopped green onion and sesame seeds.

1 cup tahini

1 1/2 cups water

1 clove garlic, minced

1 tablespoon grated ginger

3 tablespoons soy sauce

2 tablespoons rice vinegar

1 tablespoon toasted sesame oil

Combine the tahini and water in a blender and process until homogenous. Add the garlic, ginger, soy sauce, rice vinegar, and sesame oil, and pulse briefly to combine.

MOLE

Although we tend to think of mole sauce as a chile sauce with tomatoes and chocolate, in Mexico there are many variations, some of them containing no chocolate or tomatoes whatsoever. In fact, the familiar dish guacamole is yet another mole—made with avocados. This simple and fairly traditional version is tasty on enchiladas, or you can mix it into cooked beans. You can also toss veggies in it and then roast them.

1 cup commercial red salsa, or Red Chile Salsa (page 38)

2 tablespoons diced green chiles, fresh or canned

1 tablespoon unsweetened cocoa

1 tablespoon chili powder

$\frac{1}{2}$ teaspoon raw sugar

Pinch of ground cinnamon

Combine all of the ingredients in a food processor or blender and process until smooth.

PEANUT SAUCE

MAKES ABOUT 2 CUPS

This sauce goes exceptionally well with rice noodles. It's also a traditional dipping sauce for Spring Rolls (page 15). Alternately, you can toss it with steamed veggies and serve it over rice. Make sure you use natural, unsweetened peanut butter in this recipe.

1 cup peanut butter, crunchy or smooth

1 cup water

1 clove garlic, minced

1 tablespoon grated ginger

3 tablespoons soy sauce

2 tablespoons freshly squeezed lime juice

2 tablespoons coconut milk

Combine the peanut butter and water in a blender and process until smooth. Add the garlic, ginger, soy sauce, lime juice, and coconut milk, and pulse briefly to combine.

ALMOND-ORANGE SAUCE

MAKES ABOUT 1 1/2 CUPS

The orange juice gives this recipe a light, unusual flavor. Toss it with steamed veggies and serve it over rice or rice noodles.

1/2 cup raw almonds, with skins

1 teaspoon grated ginger

1/2 cup freshly squeezed orange juice

1/2 cup water

2 tablespoons soy sauce

1 tablespoon rice vinegar

Chop the almonds in a food processor, then mix in the remaining ingredients. Process until smooth.

TERIYAKI MARINADE

MAKES ABOUT 1 1/2 CUPS

Marinate veggies, tofu, tempeh, or seitan in this sauce, then roast on a greased baking sheet at 400°F, until they start to brown. Use just enough marinade to coat the veggies, and serve the extra marinade on the side as a dipping sauce.

1 cup soy sauce

1/2 cup rice vinegar

2 teaspoons raw sugar

1 clove garlic, minced

1 teaspoon grated ginger

Combine all of the ingredients and whisk until the sugar is dissolved.

VEGAN WORCESTERSHIRE SAUCE

MAKES ²/₃ CUP

This recipe works well in any Cajun-style recipe. It's also a tasty marinade for veggies, tofu, tempeh, or seitan. You can find tamarind concentrate in Indian markets, and sometimes Asian markets or natural food stores. Use just enough marinade to coat the veggies, and serve the extra marinade on the side as a dipping sauce.

½ cup water

1 teaspoon grated ginger

¼ cup soy sauce

2 tablespoons molasses

1 tablespoon tamarind concentrate

Combine the water and ginger in a small saucepan over high heat, bring to a boil, then lower the heat to maintain a gentle boil and cook for 10 minutes.

Strain the liquid and discard the ginger. Add the soy sauce, molasses, and tamarind and stir until homogenous.

BASIL MAYONNAISE

MAKES 1 CUP

I've been caught, on occasion, eating this tasty green-flecked condiment with a spoon. For a special treat, serve it with Deep-Fried Artichoke Hearts (page 20). These days, you can find quite a few different versions of vegan mayonnaise. Look for them in the refrigerated section, as well as in the condiment aisle.

1 cup vegan mayonnaise

2 tablespoons chopped basil

1 clove garlic, minced

Combine all of the ingredients in a small bowl and stir until thoroughly combined.

TOMATILLO SALSA

MAKES ABOUT 2½ CUPS

Tomatillos aren't unripe tomatoes, but rather cousins of tomatoes. They're a little tart and make for a light, refreshing salsa. You can use fresh tomatillos and fresh chiles in this recipe, if you prefer. Use 1 pound of tomatillos and 3 Anaheim chiles. Peel the papery outer skins off the tomatillos, rinse them well, then rub the tomatillos and chiles with a bit of olive oil and roast at 400°F for about 45 minutes, until they're droopy. When they're cool enough to handle, trim away the stem ends from the tomatillos and the stems from the chiles, then puree the roasted veggies along with the remaining ingredients.

2 cups canned crushed tomatillos

1 (4-ounce) can diced mild green chiles

1 cup loosely packed cilantro, stemmed and coarsely chopped

3 tablespoons red wine vinegar

1 teaspoon sea salt

Mix all of the ingredients together. Serve chilled or at room temperature.

RED CHILE SALSA

MAKES ABOUT 1 CUP

We tend to think of chiles primarily as providing heat, but they actually have plenty of flavor in addition to their spiciness. This salsa has a bit of a kick, but it relies mainly on the rich, subtle taste of ancho chiles, a dried, medium-hot pepper. Use this as an enchilada sauce, or just enjoy it with chips.

6 ancho chiles

3 tomatoes, quartered

$\frac{1}{2}$ cup chopped cilantro

3 tablespoons red wine vinegar

1 teaspoon sea salt

Soak the chiles in boiling water for at least 10 minutes. Drain them and remove the stems. Leave the seeds if you want a hotter salsa; remove them if you want it milder. Wear gloves when you take out the seeds or wash your hands right after you handle them, especially if you wear contact lenses.

Put the chiles in a food processor or blender, add the tomatoes, cilantro, vinegar, and salt, and puree until smooth.

TAMARIND-DATE CHUTNEY

MAKES ABOUT 1 CUP

Tamarind brings a perfect balance of sweet and sour to this sauce, which is a nice condiment for any curry or Indian meal. Tamarind concentrate is available in Indian markets, and sometimes in Asian markets or natural food stores.

1 cup water

$1/2$ cup pitted dates

1 tablespoon grated ginger

1 tablespoon tamarind concentrate

Combine the water, dates, and ginger in a small saucepan over medium-low heat and cook, stirring often, for 20 to 30 minutes, until the dates start to break down.

Stir in the tamarind and serve warm or chilled.

FAUX CHEESE

MAKES ABOUT 4 CUPS

Use this sauce on top of baked pasta dishes or enchiladas. If you haven't eaten cheese recently, this will taste a little like it. Either way, it works well with any tomato sauce or salsa, especially in baked dishes like lasagna and enchiladas. And it tastes much better than it sounds, I promise! Although the ingredient list calls for whole wheat pastry flour, you can use any flour that you have on hand.

1 tablespoon olive oil

$1/2$ cup whole wheat pastry flour

$1/2$ cup nutritional yeast, preferably large flake

3 cups water

1 teaspoon sea salt

1 teaspoon prepared mustard

Gently heat the oil in a saucepan over medium-low heat, then whisk in the flour and nutritional yeast, turn the heat down to low, and cook, whisking constantly, for a minute or two, until the mixture is reasonably homogenous, with few lumps. Add the water, raise the heat to medium, and bring the mixture to a boil, whisking until it's relatively smooth. Simmer for 2 to 3 minutes, until the mixture thickens to the consistency of pea soup, then remove it from the heat and whisk in the salt and mustard.

SALADS AND DRESSINGS

GREEN SALAD WITH ADDITIONS

I'm an avid fan of salad mix. Prepared, prewashed salad mix has a much wider variety of greens than most of us would have access to if we shopped for the greens individually. You can almost always find a packaged variety, and many supermarkets also sell mixed salad greens in bulk in their produce sections. Look for salad mix at farmers' markets, as well.

4 cups mixed greens

1 ripe tomato, chopped

1 red bell pepper, chopped

$\frac{1}{2}$ cup chopped radishes

1 cucumber, peeled and chopped

3 to 4 tablespoons salad dressing of your choice (pages 46–48)

$\frac{1}{2}$ cup Croutons (page 44)

2 tablespoons Tamari-Roasted Sunflower Seeds (page 45)

Put the greens, tomato, bell pepper, radishes, and cucumber in a salad bowl, drizzle the salad dressing over, and toss to combine and coat the veggies with the dressing. Sprinkle the croutons and sunflower seeds over the salad and toss lightly before serving.

CROUTONS

Croutons are an excellent way to make use of stale bread. In fact, stale bread works best here. Since the bread cubes sit out for a day before making the croutons, plan ahead.

4 slices hearty whole wheat bread

$1\frac{1}{2}$ tablespoons olive oil

$\frac{1}{2}$ teaspoon sea salt

1 teaspoon dried basil

Cut the bread into bite-sized chunks and let it sit out overnight to dry.

Preheat the oven to 350°F.

Toss the dried bread chunks with the oil, salt, and basil, then spread them in an even layer on a cookie sheet. Bake for about 20 minutes, until the croutons are golden brown.

TAMARI-ROASTED SUNFLOWER SEEDS

MAKES 1 CUP

On hot days when you don't want to turn on your oven, you can roast the sunflower seeds in a skillet over high heat for a minute or two, then stir in the soy sauce and turn off the heat right away.

1 cup raw sunflower seeds

2 tablespoons tamari or soy sauce, or more to taste

Preheat the oven to 375°F.

Toss the sunflower seeds with the soy sauce, then spread them in an even layer in a small baking pan or pie pan. Bake for about 20 minutes, until they're aromatic.

MUSTARD VINAIGRETTE DRESSING

MAKES 4 TO 6 SERVINGS

Use a good olive oil in this recipe. You'll taste the difference.

1/2 cup red wine vinegar

1/4 cup extra-virgin olive oil

1 teaspoon Dijon or Poupon mustard

1/2 teaspoon dried dill

1/2 teaspoon dried tarragon

1/2 teaspoon dried basil

1/2 teaspoon sea salt

1/2 teaspoon freshly ground black pepper

Whisk all of the ingredients together until emulsified, or combine everything in a jar with a tight-fitting lid and shake until emulsified. Taste a bit on a lettuce leaf and add more salt if you like.

TOMATO-BASIL SALAD DRESSING

This no-oil dressing takes only a moment to prepare.

1 cup tomato juice

10 to 12 basil leaves, minced

1 tablespoon balsamic vinegar

Whisk all of the ingredients together, or combine everything in a jar with a tight-fitting lid and shake to mix.

TAHINI DRESSING

This rich salad dressing is also a great sauce for steamed veggies.

$1/2$ cup tahini

1 tablespoon freshly squeezed lemon juice, or more to taste

1 tablespoon extra-virgin olive oil

1 tablespoon chopped fresh or 1 teaspoon dried parsley

1 clove garlic, minced

$1/2$ teaspoon sea salt

$3/4$ cup water

Combine the tahini, lemon juice, olive oil, parsley, garlic, and salt in a food processor or blender and process briefly to mix. Slowly add the water and process until smooth and thoroughly blended.

MARINATED POTATO SALAD

MAKES 6 SERVINGS

This almost traditional potato salad includes fresh dill for an extra dimension of flavor.

2 pounds red potatoes (unpeeled)

$1/2$ cup red onion, finely chopped

4 pickles, cut in bite-sized pieces

3 tablespoons chopped dill

2 tablespoons red wine vinegar

1 tablespoon prepared mustard

1 tablespoon extra-virgin olive oil

1 teaspoon sea salt

$1/2$ teaspoon freshly ground black pepper

Chop the potatoes into bite-sized chunks, put them in a saucepan with enough water to cover by an inch or two, and boil for about 10 minutes, until soft.

Drain the potatoes, transfer to a bowl, and stir in the red onion, pickles, and dill. In a separate small bowl, combine the vinegar, mustard, olive oil, salt, and pepper and whisk until emulsified. Pour the dressing over the potatoes and mix well. Taste and add more salt if you like. Let stand for at least 30 minutes for the flavor to develop, then serve at room temperature or chilled.

GREEN BEAN AND ALMOND SALAD

MAKES 4 SERVINGS

Make this salad in high summer, when green beans are at their peak.

8 ounces green beans, trimmed and halved crosswise

10 to 12 cherry tomatoes, cut in quarters

$1/4$ cup slivered almonds

2 tablespoons red wine or balsamic vinegar

1 tablespoon extra-virgin olive oil

1 teaspoon dried dill

$1/2$ teaspoon sea salt

Freshly ground black pepper

Bring a saucepan of water to a rolling boil, then add the green beans and blanch for 30 seconds. Drain immediately and rinse with cold water.

Put the green beans in a bowl and stir in the tomatoes and almonds. In a separate small bowl, combine the vinegar, olive oil, dill, and salt and whisk until emulsified. Pour the dressing over the green beans and mix well. Season to taste with pepper, and more salt if you like. Let stand for at least 10 minutes for the flavors to develop, and serve at room temperature.

MARINATED CUCUMBER SALAD

MAKES 2 CUPS

I make this salad when I crave something green—and inexpensive. I never get tired of it.

2 tablespoons red wine vinegar

1 tablespoon extra-virgin olive oil

1 teaspoon dried dill

1/8 teaspoon sea salt

Pinch of freshly ground black pepper

1 large cucumber, peeled and chopped

Combine the vinegar, olive oil, dill, salt, and pepper in a serving bowl and whisk until emulsified. Gently stir in the cucumber. Let stand for 10 minutes for the flavors to develop, and serve at room temperature.

ASIAN CUCUMBER SALAD

Serve this as a fresh, raw vegetable complement to Yakisoba (page 100).

2 tablespoons soy sauce

1 tablespoon rice vinegar

1 teaspoon grated ginger

1 tablespoon black sesame seeds

Pinch of raw sugar

1 cucumber, peeled and sliced

Combine the soy sauce, vinegar, ginger, sesame seeds, and sugar in a serving bowl and whisk to combine. Gently stir in the cucumber. Let stand for 10 minutes for the flavors to develop, and serve at room temperature.

CORN AND GREEN BEAN SALAD

MAKES 4 SERVINGS

This is a colorful salad of marinated veggies accented with sun-dried tomatoes and sunflower seeds. You can substitute broccoli or asparagus for the green beans. The corn will thaw almost immediately when you mix it with the other ingredients.

8 to 10 sun-dried tomatoes

1 cup frozen corn kernels

2 cups green beans, trimmed and halved crosswise

2 ripe tomatoes, chopped

1/2 red onion, chopped

1/4 cup raw sunflower seeds

2 tablespoons chopped basil

1 tablespoon balsamic vinegar

1 tablespoon extra-virgin olive oil

1 teaspoon dried marjoram

1 teaspoon sea salt

Freshly ground black pepper

Soak the sun-dried tomatoes in boiling water for a few minutes, until softened.

Drain the tomatoes, chop them finely, then put them in a serving bowl and stir in the corn, green beans, tomatoes, onion, sunflower seeds, and basil. In a separate small bowl, combine the vinegar, olive oil, marjoram, and sea salt and whisk until emulsified. Pour the dressing over the salad and mix well. Season to taste with pepper before serving. Let stand for 10 minutes for the flavors to develop, and serve at room temperature.

KIM CHEE

MAKES 6 SERVINGS

This spicy coleslaw goes well with Korean Barbecued Seitan (page 154). It will be tasty after marinating for a day, and even better if you leave it a few days longer.

1 cup rice vinegar

1 teaspoon sea salt

1 teaspoon raw sugar

1 tablespoon crushed red pepper, or to taste

1 onion, cut in rings

2 cloves garlic, minced

1 tablespoon grated ginger

1 cup water

1 small head napa cabbage

2 carrots, grated

1 cup grated daikon radish

Combine the vinegar, salt, sugar, and crushed red pepper in a small saucepan and stir over medium-high heat until the salt and sugar dissolve. Stir in the onion, garlic, ginger, and water, bring to a boil, then turn off the heat, and let stand for 5 minutes.

Combine the cabbage, carrots, and daikon in a serving bowl, pour the marinade over the veggies, and mix well. Store the kim chee in an airtight container in the refrigerator for at least a day, mixing it every few hours. Serve chilled or at room temperature.

MEXICAN TOMATO SALAD

This salad provides a good counterpoint to Mexican dishes full of beans, like Tamale Pie (page 122) or Enchilada Pie (page 124). The corn will thaw almost immediately when you mix it with the other ingredients.

4 ripe tomatoes, chopped

1 zucchini, chopped

1 cup frozen corn kernels

1/4 cup chopped raw almonds, with skins

2 tablespoons diced mild green chiles, fresh or canned

1 tablespoon chopped cilantro

2 tablespoons red wine vinegar

1 tablespoon extra-virgin olive oil

1 teaspoon chili powder, mild or hot

1/2 teaspoon ground cumin

1/2 teaspoon dried oregano

1/2 teaspoon sea salt

Combine the tomatoes, zucchini, corn, almonds, green chiles, and cilantro in a serving bowl. In a separate small bowl, combine the vinegar, olive oil, chili powder, cumin, oregano, and salt and whisk until emulsified. Pour the dressing over the veggies and mix well. Taste and add more salt if you like. Serve at room temperature.

GREEK SALAD

I love pickled, salty foods. This salad is full of them, along with plenty of fresh veggies for balance. Pepperoncini, or Greek pickled peppers, add a slightly sweet, tart flavor, and a bit of heat, as well.

1 cucumber, peeled and chopped

1 ripe tomato, chopped

1 carrot, chopped

8 to 10 pepperoncini

12 to 15 pitted kalamata olives

1 (14-ounce) can quartered artichoke hearts, drained

2 to 3 tablespoons red wine vinegar

1 to 2 tablespoons extra-virgin olive oil

1 teaspoon dried dill

$1/2$ teaspoon dried oregano

Sea salt

Freshly ground black pepper

Combine the cucumber, tomato, carrot, pepperoncini, olives, and artichoke hearts in a serving bowl. In a separate small bowl, combine the vinegar, olive oil, dill, and oregano and whisk until emulsified. Pour the dressing over the veggies and mix well, then season to taste with salt and pepper. Let stand for 10 minutes for the flavors to develop, and serve at room temperature.

SPINACH-BASIL PASTA SALAD

This is a colorful, summery salad. The fresh spinach makes it especially vibrant. Spiral or tubular pasta work best in this recipe.

1 pound colorful pasta

1 bunch fresh spinach, cleaned and stemmed

2 ripe tomatoes, chopped

¼ cup chopped basil

¼ cup sliced black olives

3 tablespoons red wine vinegar or balsamic vinegar

1 tablespoon extra-virgin olive oil

1 teaspoon sea salt

Freshly ground black pepper

Bring a large pot of salted water to a boil over medium-high heat, stir in the pasta, and cook, stirring often, for 8 to 10 minutes, until al dente.

Drain the pasta in a colander, then cool by running cold water through it. Shake the colander to shed the excess water. Put the pasta in a serving bowl and stir in the spinach, tomatoes, basil, and olives. In a separate small bowl, combine the vinegar, olive oil, and salt and whisk to emulsify. Pour the dressing over the pasta salad, mix well, and season to taste with pepper. Let stand for 10 minutes for the flavors to develop, and serve at room temperature.

SPINACH AND POPPY SEED PASTA SALAD

Chives are members of the onion family with a light, summery flavor that goes well with almost anything, They're especially good raw. Tubular or spiral pasta work best in this recipe.

1 pound colorful pasta

1 bunch spinach, cleaned and stemmed

$1/2$ red onion, chopped

2 tablespoons chopped chives

3 tablespoons poppy seeds

2 tablespoons freshly squeezed lemon juice

2 tablespoons extra-virgin olive oil

1 teaspoon sea salt

Freshly ground black pepper

Bring a large pot of salted water to a boil over medium-high heat, stir in the pasta, and cook, stirring often, for 8 to 10 minutes, until al dente.

Drain the pasta in a colander, then cool by running cold water through it. Shake the colander to shed the excess water. Put the pasta in a serving bowl and stir in the spinach, onion, chives, and poppy seeds. In a separate small bowl, combine the lemon juice, olive oil, and salt and whisk until emulsified. Pour the dressing over the pasta salad, mix well, and season to taste with pepper. Let stand for 10 minutes for the flavors to develop, and serve at room temperature.

SZECHUAN NOODLE SALAD

I love cool, spicy food on hot days. If you don't like piquant flavors, you can reduce the amount of chili oil or leave it out altogether. You can find black sesame seeds in Asian markets, and sometimes at natural food stores.

1 pound capellini or angel hair pasta

1 cup grated daikon radish

2 carrots, grated

1 cup snow peas, trimmed and halved

3 tablespoons soy sauce

2 tablespoons rice vinegar

1 teaspoon toasted sesame oil

1 teaspoon chili oil, or more to taste

1/2 teaspoon raw sugar

3 green onions, chopped

2 tablespoons black sesame seeds

Bring a large pot of salted water to a boil over medium-high heat, stir in the pasta, and cook, stirring often, for 8 to 10 minutes, until al dente.

Drain the pasta in a colander, then cool by running cold water through it. Shake the colander to shed the excess water. Put the pasta in a serving bowl and gently fold in the daikon, carrots, and snow peas. In a separate small bowl, combine the soy sauce, vinegar, sesame oil, chili oil, and sugar and whisk until the sugar is dissolved. Toss this dressing with the noodles and veggies. Sprinkle the green onions and sesame seeds over the salad before serving. Serve chilled or at room temperature.

CASHEW-ARAME NOODLE SALAD

Arame, a sea vegetable that looks like fine black noodles, contrasts nicely with the white noodles and grated carrots in this recipe. You can buy arame in natural food stores. I like to make this salad around Halloween because of the black and orange color combination, which is fairly unusual in the world of food.

1 pound thin rice noodles

3 ounces dried arame

1 teaspoon olive oil

$\frac{1}{2}$ onion, chopped

2 cloves garlic, minced

1 tablespoon grated ginger

$\frac{1}{2}$ cup soy sauce

$\frac{1}{4}$ cup rice vinegar

$\frac{1}{2}$ teaspoon raw sugar

2 carrots, grated

$\frac{1}{2}$ cup salted, roasted cashew pieces

Put the rice noodles in a bowl, pour in boiling water to cover by a couple of inches, and soak the noodles for about 10 minutes, until they're just soft. Soak the arame in warm water to cover by a couple of inches for 5 to 10 minutes.

Drain the noodles in a colander, then cool by running cold water through them. Shake the colander to shed the extra water.

Meanwhile, heat the oil in a small saucepan over medium-low heat, add the onion, garlic, and ginger, and saute for about 5 minutes, until the onion is soft.

Combine the soy sauce, rice vinegar, and sugar in a small bowl and stir to dissolve the sugar. Drain the arame, put it in a serving bowl, and stir in the carrots. Add the rice noodles, then pour in the sauce and the onion mixture and gently stir to combine. Serve topped with the cashews. Let stand for 10 minutes for the flavors to develop and serve chilled or at room temperature.

VIETNAMESE NOODLE SALAD

MAKES 6 SERVINGS

The traditional Vietnamese flavors of basil, mint, and lime combine to make a complex and refreshing dressing for this rice noodle salad. Feel free to experiment with the veggies, adding whatever you'd like.

8 ounces thin rice noodles

2 carrots, grated

1 ripe tomato, chopped

1 cup finely chopped bok choy

$\frac{1}{2}$ cup bean sprouts

$\frac{1}{2}$ cup snow peas, trimmed and halved crosswise

2 tablespoons chopped Thai basil (see Pantry, page 208)

2 tablespoons chopped mint

1 teaspoon grated ginger

3 tablespoons soy sauce

2 tablespoons freshly squeezed lime juice

Put the rice noodles in a bowl, pour in boiling water to cover by a couple of inches, and soak the noodles for about 10 minutes, until they're just soft.

Drain the noodles in a colander, then cool by running cold water through them. Shake the colander to shed the excess water. Put the noodles in a serving bowl, add the carrots, tomato, bok choy, sprouts, snow peas, basil, mint, and ginger and toss with tongs to combine. Add the soy sauce and lime juice and stir gently until all the ingredients are evenly coated. It'll be tasty right away, and even better in 10 minutes.

THAI NOODLE SALAD

I owned a wholesale business for a while, selling prepared food to grocery stores, food co-ops, and university cafeterias. This was our most popular item

8 ounces thin rice noodles

1 cup Peanut Sauce (page 32)

1 cup shredded red cabbage

1 bunch green onions, chopped

½ cup chopped roasted peanuts

Put the rice noodles in a bowl, pour in boiling water to cover by a couple of inches, and soak the noodles for 10 minutes, until they're just soft.

Drain the noodles in a colander, then cool by running cold water through them. Shake the colander to shed the excess water.

Put the rice noodles in a serving bowl, pour in the peanut sauce, and stir gently to combine. Scatter the cabbage, green onions, and peanuts on top before serving. It'll be tasty right away, and even better in 10 minutes.

LEBANESE WHITE BEAN SALAD

MAKES 4 TO 6 SERVINGS

I like a salad with plenty of protein. This one makes a refreshing meal all on its own, or you can serve it with Spanakopita (page 131) or Seitan Gyros (page 157).

2 cups cooked white beans, or 1 (15-ounce) can, drained

1 cucumber, peeled and chopped

1 ripe tomato, chopped

1 tablespoon chopped fresh dill, or 1 teaspoon dried dill

1 tablespoon chopped fresh mint, or 1 teaspoon dried mint

1 tablespoon freshly squeezed lemon juice, or more to taste

1 tablespoon extra-virgin olive oil

1 teaspoon ground cumin

$\frac{1}{2}$ teaspoon sea salt

Freshly ground black pepper

Combine the beans, cucumber, tomato, dill, and mint in a serving bowl.

In a separate small bowl, combine the lemon juice, olive oil, cumin, and salt and whisk until emulsified. Pour the dressing over the salad and mix well. Season to taste with pepper, and more salt if you like. Let stand for 10 minutes for the flavors to develop. Serve at room temperature.

CURRIED CHICKPEA SALAD

Chickpeas work particularly well in salads because they keep their shape and soak up plenty of flavor. You can substitute 2½ teaspoons of curry powder for the cumin, turmeric, cardamom, and coriander. In fact, any time you see a list of spices in one of my Indian recipes you can use an equal amount of curry powder, which is just a blend of spices. Choosing the spices individually gives you more control over the flavor, but it'll taste good either way. You can also toast the spices by cooking them in a dry skillet over low heat for a minute or two, which helps bring out their flavor. But again, the dish will be tasty even if you don't take the extra step.

3 cups cooked chickpeas, or 1½ (15-ounce) cans, drained

3 ripe tomatoes, chopped

1 tablespoon chopped mint

1 teaspoon grated ginger

1 tablespoon freshly squeezed lemon juice

1 tablespoon extra-virgin olive oil (optional)

1 teaspoon ground cumin

½ teaspoon ground turmeric

½ teaspoon ground cardamom

½ teaspoon ground coriander

1 teaspoon sea salt

Put all of the ingredients in a serving bowl and stir until thoroughly combined. Taste and add more salt if you like. Let stand for 10 minutes for the flavors to develop. Serve at room temperature.

BLACK BEAN AND CORN SALAD

Serve this salad with any variety of Tamales (pages 118–121) for a satisfying, nutritious meal. The corn will thaw almost immediately when you mix it with the other ingredients.

2 cups cooked black beans, or 1 (15-ounce) can, drained and rinsed

2 ripe tomatoes, chopped

1 red bell pepper, cut in strips (optional)

$\frac{1}{2}$ red onion, chopped

1 cup frozen corn kernels

1 (4-ounce) can diced mild green chiles

2 tablespoons chopped cilantro

2 tablespoons freshly squeezed lime juice

1 tablespoon extra-virgin olive oil

1 teaspoon chili powder, mild or hot

$\frac{1}{2}$ teaspoon ground cumin

$\frac{1}{2}$ teaspoon dried oregano

Sea salt

Cayenne

Put the beans, tomatoes, bell pepper, onion, corn, green chiles, cilantro, lime juice, olive oil, chili powder, cumin, and oregano in a serving bowl and stir until thoroughly combined. Season to taste with salt and cayenne. Let stand for 10 minutes for the flavors to develop. Serve at room temperature.

CARIBBEAN BLACK-EYED PEA SALAD

The combination of allspice and thyme is a classic Caribbean flavoring that's both sweet and savory.

2 cup cooked black-eyed peas, or 1 (15-ounce) can, drained

2 cups cooked brown rice, chilled

2 ripe tomatoes, chopped

2 stalks celery, finely chopped

$\frac{1}{2}$ cup sliced green olives

3 tablespoons red wine vinegar

1 tablespoon extra-virgin olive oil

1 teaspoon dried thyme

$\frac{1}{2}$ teaspoon ground allspice

1 teaspoon sea salt

Hot sauce

Combine the black-eyed peas, rice, tomatoes, celery, and olives in a serving bowl. In a separate small bowl, combine the vinegar, olive oil, thyme, allspice, and salt and whisk until emulsified. Pour the dressing over the salad and mix well.

Season to taste with hot sauce. Let stand for 10 minutes for the flavors to develop. Serve chilled, or at room temperature.

ANTIPASTO SALAD

MAKES 6 SERVINGS

Serve this Italian salad with pasta or lasagna. A traditional antipasto plate is an arrangement of tasty appetizers, including a variety of cured meats. My version omits the meat, of course, and has all the other ingredients mixed together. You can use less oil for a lower-fat version.

2 cups cooked chickpeas, or 1 (15-ounce) can, drained

8 to 10 canned artichoke hearts, drained

12 to 15 pitted kalamata olives

8 to 10 pepperoncini

1 (8-ounce) jar roasted red bell peppers, drained and cut in strips

2 tablespoons red wine vinegar

2 tablespoons extra-virgin olive oil

1 teaspoon dried basil

$\frac{1}{2}$ teaspoon dried oregano

$\frac{1}{2}$ teaspoon dried marjoram

$\frac{1}{2}$ teaspoon dried tarragon

Sea salt

Freshly ground black pepper

Combine the chickpeas, artichoke hearts, olives, pepperoncini, and pepper strips in a serving bowl. In a separate small bowl, combine the vinegar, olive oil, basil, oregano, marjoram, and tarragon and whisk until emulsified. Pour the dressing over the salad and mix well. Season to taste with salt and pepper. Let stand for 10 minutes for the flavors to develop. Serve chilled, or at room temperature.

TABOULEH

MAKES 4 SERVINGS

This classic Middle Eastern bulgur wheat salad works well with Hummus (page 2), Baba Ghanoush (page 6), and Dolmades (page 18). Serve it all with pita bread. You can use more olive oil if you prefer a richer salad.

1 cup bulgur wheat

1½ cups boiling water

2 ripe tomatoes, chopped

3 green onions, chopped

1 bunch parsley, stemmed and chopped

1 tablespoon chopped mint

2 tablespoons freshly squeezed lemon juice, or more to taste

1 tablespoon extra-virgin olive oil

1 tablespoon red wine vinegar

1 teaspoon sea salt

½ teaspoon freshly ground black pepper

Put the bulgur in a serving bowl, pour in the water, and let sit for about 15 minutes, until all of the water is absorbed.

Stir in the tomatoes, green onions, parsley, and mint. In a separate small bowl, combine the lemon juice, olive oil, vinegar, salt, and pepper, and whisk until emulsified. Pour the dressing over the salad and mix well. Let stand for 30 minutes and serve at room temperature.

WILD RICE SALAD WITH SUN-DRIED TOMATOES

MAKES 4 TO 6 SERVINGS

This hearty, satisfying salad features a wide range of flavors and textures. Serve it with Curried Squash Soup (page 84).

$3\frac{1}{2}$ cups water

$\frac{1}{2}$ cup wild rice

1 cup brown rice

10 to 12 sun-dried tomatoes

$\frac{1}{2}$ cup sliced green olives

$\frac{1}{4}$ cup raw sunflower seeds

2 tablespoons chopped parsley

2 tablespoons red wine vinegar

1 tablespoon extra-virgin olive oil

1 teaspoon prepared mustard

1 teaspoon dried rosemary leaf

1 teaspoon salt

$\frac{1}{2}$ teaspoon anise seed

Bring the water to a boil in a saucepan over high heat. Stir in the wild rice, turn the heat down to medium-low, cover, and cook for 30 minutes. Stir in the brown rice, lower the heat, cover, and simmer for about 45 minutes longer, until all of the liquid is absorbed.

Meanwhile, soak the sun-dried tomatoes in boiling water for a few minutes, until softened. Drain and slice the tomatoes, then put them in a serving bowl with the olives, sunflower seeds, and parsley. In a separate small bowl, combine the vinegar, olive oil, mustard, rosemary, salt, and anise and whisk until emulsified.

When the rice is ready, transfer it to a sieve, then cool by running cold water through it. Shake the colander to shed the excess water. Add it to the serving bowl, pour in the dressing (rewhisking if needed), and mix well. Let sit for 10 minutes for the flavors to develop. Serve chilled, or at room temperature.

SPELT AND TOMATO SALAD

MAKES 4 TO 6 SERVINGS

Although spelt is an ancient relative of wheat, many people who are allergic to wheat are able to tolerate spelt. Cooked spelt berries are crunchy on the outside and soft on the inside, and in this salad they do a wonderful job of carrying the flavor of the basil and balsamic vinegar. You can find spelt berries (and other spelt products) in natural food stores.

2 cups water

1 cup spelt berries

2 ripe tomatoes, chopped

2 tablespoons chopped basil

2 tablespoons balsamic vinegar

1 tablespoon extra-virgin olive oil

1/2 teaspoon sea salt

Bring the water to a boil in a small saucepan over high heat, then stir in the spelt berries, lower the heat, cover, and simmer for about 30 to 40 minutes, until the water is absorbed.

Transfer the spelt to a sieve, then cool by running cold water through it. Shake the colander to shed excess water. Put the spelt in a serving bowl and stir in the tomatoes and basil. In a separate small bowl, combine the balsamic vinegar, olive oil, and salt and whisk until emulsified. Pour the dressing over the salad and mix well, then taste and add more salt if you like. Let sit for 10 minutes for the flavors to develop. Serve at room temperature.

COUSCOUS SALAD

MAKES 6 SERVINGS

Couscous is a tiny pasta made from semolina, a variety of wheat widely used in North Africa and southern France. The frozen peas will thaw almost immediately when you mix them with the other ingredients.

2 cups couscous

3 cups boiling water

1 cup frozen peas

1 cup grated carrots

$1/4$ cup chopped parsley

$1/4$ cup chopped or slivered almonds

2 tablespoons freshly squeezed lemon juice, or more to taste

2 tablespoons extra-virgin olive oil

1 teaspoon ground cumin

1 teaspoon dried mint

1 teaspoon sea salt

$1/2$ teaspoon freshly ground black pepper

Put the couscous in a serving bowl, pour in the water, and let sit for 10 to 15 minutes, until all of the water is absorbed.

Stir in the peas, carrots, parsley, and almonds. In a separate small bowl, combine the lemon juice, olive oil, cumin, mint, salt, and pepper, and whisk to emulsify. Pour the dressing over the salad and mix well. Let stand for 10 minutes for the flavors to develop. Serve chilled, or at room temperature.

SOUPS

VEGGIE STOCK

MAKES 3 TO 4 QUARTS

There is no question that the best soups start with lovingly prepared stock that simmers for hours, yet it's been my experience that you can also make tasty soup without fussing over the stock. If you don't have the time to prepare stock in advance, you can start with water and add a parsnip to your broth, then pull the parsnip out at the end. You can use a couple of strips of kombu (a type of kelp available in natural food stores) in the same way. If you do have time to make stock, here's a basic recipe that uses plenty of flavorful vegetables.

4 quarts water

1 carrot, coarsely chopped

1 onion, coarsely chopped

1 potato, coarsely chopped

1 parsnip, coarsely chopped

2 cloves garlic

1 teaspoon sea salt

1 teaspoon freshly ground black pepper

Combine all of the ingredients in a stockpot over high heat, bring to a boil, then lower the heat and simmer for 1 to 2 hours. Strain the stock and discard the veggies. Stored in an airtight container, the stock will keep for 1 week in the refrigerator or several months in the freezer.

QUICK TOMATO SOUP

MAKES 4 TO 6 SERVINGS

You can make this soup in 15 to 20 minutes if you have cooked rice on hand. It's a favorite at my restaurant, especially among the staff.

1 tablespoon olive oil

1 onion, chopped

1 stalk celery, chopped

1 (48-ounce) can tomato juice

1 cup frozen peas

1 teaspoon dried dill

1 teaspoon sea salt

1/2 teaspoon freshly ground black pepper

1 cup cooked brown rice

Heat the oil in a soup pot over medium-low heat, add the onion and celery, and sauté for about 5 minutes, until the onion is soft. Stir in the tomato juice, peas, dill, salt, and pepper, and cook, uncovered, another 10 to 15 minutes, stirring occasionally, until it's heated through. Stir in the rice, cook until heated through, and serve hot.

THAI TOMATO SOUP

MAKES 6 TO 8 SERVINGS

This soup is creamy, tangy, and simple. Serve it with Spinach and Tofu in Peanut Sauce (page 148) or Thai Curry with Seitan (page 152).

2 cups Veggie Stock (page 74) or water

2 cups chopped bok choy

1/4 cup chopped Thai basil (see Pantry, page 208)

1 tablespoon grated ginger

1 (48-ounce) can tomato juice

3 tablespoons soy sauce, or more to taste

1 cup bean sprouts

1/2 cup coconut milk

2 tablespoons freshly squeezed lime juice

Combine the stock, bok choy, basil, and ginger in a soup pot over medium-low heat and cook for 10 minutes. Stir in the tomato juice, soy sauce, and sprouts, cover, and cook another 10 minutes, until all of the vegetables are tender. Stir in the coconut milk and lime juice, and serve hot.

MEXICAN TOMATO SOUP

MAKES 6 SERVINGS

Add hot sauce (see Pantry, page 210) or a minced chipotle chile to make this south-of-the border soup hotter, if you'd like.

1 tablespoon olive oil

2 cloves garlic, minced

2 tablespoons chopped cilantro

1 (48-ounce) can tomato juice

1 cup frozen corn kernels

1 (4-ounce) can diced mild green chiles

1½ tablespoons freshly squeezed lime juice

1 teaspoon sea salt

Crushed tortilla chips for garnish

Heat the oil in a soup pot over medium-low heat, add the garlic and cilantro, and sauté for a minute or two. Stir in the tomato juice, corn, chiles, lime juice, and salt, bring to a boil, then lower the heat, cover, and simmer for 15 minutes. Serve hot, topped with the tortilla chips.

GAZPACHO

This perfect summer soup is fat free and refreshing. For optimum flavor, use juicy, perfectly ripe tomatoes.

4 ripe tomatoes, coarsely chopped

1 cucumber, peeled and cut in chunks

2 tablespoons chopped tarragon

2 tablespoons chopped basil

2 cups tomato juice

2 tablespoons red wine vinegar

1 teaspoon sea salt

Hot sauce

Combine the tomatoes, cucumber, tarragon, and basil in a food processor or blender and process until smooth. Transfer the mixture to a serving bowl and whisk in the tomato juice, vinegar, and salt. Season with hot sauce to taste, and serve chilled.

MISO-NOODLE SOUP

MAKES 8 TO 10 SERVINGS

This is a hearty, satisfying soup—if a bit strange. When I first tasted a version of it, I was a bit unsettled by the kombu (a type of kelp available in natural food stores), but now I pick out those chewy pieces and eat them first. I like to make a big pot of this soup when I'm sick or after overindulging on a holiday like Halloween or New Year's, because the miso and kombu are cleansing. Any type of miso is fine here, but do use the thinner rice noodles from China in this recipe (see Pantry, page 214).

6 strips of kombu

12 cups Veggie Stock (page 74)

3 carrots, sliced

1 onion, chopped

4 cloves garlic, minced

2 tablespoons grated ginger

1/2 cup soy sauce

1 pound firm tofu, cut in small cubes

8 ounces frozen peas

8 ounces thin rice noodles

3 tablespoons miso

3 tablespoons rice vinegar

Soak the kombu in hot water for about 10 minutes, until it softens, then cut it into bite-sized pieces.

(continued)

Miso–Noodle Soup, continued

Meanwhile, bring the stock to a boil in a soup pot, then stir in the carrots, onion, garlic, ginger, and soy sauce. Lower the heat, cover, and simmer for about 15 minutes. Stir in the tofu and peas, cover, and simmer for 10 minutes longer, until the vegetables are tender.

Turn off the heat and add the rice noodles and kombu, along with its soaking liquid. Skim off a cup of stock, dissolve the miso in it, then add it to the soup along with the rice vinegar. Let the soup stand, uncovered, for about 10 minutes, until the rice noodles are soft, then serve right away.

HOT-AND-SOUR SOUP

MAKES 6 TO 8 SERVINGS

This soup has a wonderful variety of flavors and textures. Serve it with Lo Mein (page 98) or Chinese Veggies in Black Bean Sauce (page 128). You can find chili oil in natural food stores or Asian markets.

6 to 8 cups Veggie Stock (page 74)

10 mushrooms, chopped (button, shiitake, oyster, or a variety)

2 carrots, cut in thin strips

1 onion, chopped

2 or 3 cloves garlic, minced

2 tablespoons grated ginger

4 ounces firm tofu, cut in strips

1 (5-ounce) can bamboo shoot strips, drained

1 (5-ounce) can water chestnuts, drained and finely chopped

1/2 cup peas, fresh or frozen

4 tablespoons soy sauce, or to taste

3 tablespoons rice vinegar

1 tablespoon toasted sesame oil

1 teaspoon to 1 tablespoon chili oil

Bring the stock to a boil in a soup pot, then stir in the mushrooms, carrots, onion, garlic, and ginger. Lower the heat, cover, and simmer for 30 to 40 minutes, until the vegetables are tender. Stir in the tofu, bamboo shoots, water chestnuts, peas, soy sauce, and rice vinegar, and simmer another 5 minutes. Stir in the sesame and chili oils and serve hot.

SOUTHEAST ASIAN HOT-AND-SOUR SOUP WITH LEMONGRASS

MAKES 6 SERVINGS

Take the extra time to find the lemongrass and kaffir lime leaves for this soup. It's worth the effort. They're available in Asian groceries and exemplary supermarkets.

6 to 8 cups Veggie Stock (page 74)

10 to 12 mushrooms, quartered

2 tomatoes, chopped

1 onion, chopped

2 cloves garlic, chopped

1 tablespoon grated ginger

2 stalks fresh lemongrass, cut in 2-inch pieces

6 to 8 kaffir lime leaves

8 ounces firm tofu, cut in $1/2$-inch cubes

2 tablespoons chopped Thai basil (see Pantry, page 208)

2 tablespoons chopped mint

$1/2$ cup coconut milk

3 tablespoons soy sauce, or more to taste

1 tablespoon raw sugar (optional)

2 tablespoons freshly squeezed lime juice, or more to taste

Chili oil

Combine the stock, mushrooms, tomatoes, onion, garlic, ginger, lemongrass, and lime leaves in a soup pot, bring to a boil, then lower the heat to medium-low and cook, uncovered, for 30 minutes. Stir in the tofu, basil, mint, coconut milk, soy sauce, and sugar and simmer another 10 minutes. Add the lime juice, then stir in chili oil to taste. Pick out the lemongrass and lime leaves, and serve hot.

THAI PUMPKIN-COCONUT SOUP

MAKES 6 SERVINGS

This soup has a thick, creamy base and many wonderful layers of flavor.

2 acorn squash

4 cups Veggie Stock (page 74) or water

2 leeks, cleaned well and chopped

1/4 cup chopped shallots

6 cloves garlic, minced

2 tablespoons grated ginger

2 stalks lemongrass, cut in 2-inch pieces

6 kaffir lime leaves

3 tablespoons soy sauce

2 cups chopped bok choy

1 cup loosely packed Thai basil leaves (see Pantry, page 208)

1 (6-ounce) can coconut milk

Freshly squeezed juice of 1 lime

Cut the squash in half, scoop out the seeds, and cut the squash into pieces that will fit in your steamer. Steam for 30 to 40 minutes, until very soft.

Meanwhile, combine the stock, leeks, shallots, garlic, ginger, lemongrass, lime leaves, and soy sauce in a soup pot and bring to a boil. Turn the heat down to medium-low, and cook for about 30 minutes. Stir in the bok choy and basil, cook for another 10 minutes, then pick out the lemongrass and lime leaves and stir in the coconut milk and lime juice.

When the squash is soft, scoop out the flesh and puree it with a cup or two of the soup broth, then stir it back into the soup. Serve the soup hot.

CURRIED SQUASH SOUP

MAKES 6 SERVINGS

This comforting winter soup is thick enough to be filling, but surprisingly light thanks to the ginger and lemon juice.

2 acorn squash

4 cups Veggie Stock (page 74) or water

2 carrots, cut in chunks

1 onion, quartered

1 parsnip, cut in chunks

1 tablespoon grated ginger

$\frac{1}{2}$ teaspoon ground cardamom

1 teaspoon sea salt

1 tablespoon freshly squeezed lemon juice

Cut the squash in half, scoop out the seeds, and cut the squash into pieces that will fit in your steamer. Steam for 30 to 40 minutes, until very soft.

Meanwhile, bring the stock to a boil, then stir in the carrots, onion, parsnip, ginger, cardamom, and salt. Lower the heat, cover, and simmer for 20 minutes, until the vegetables are barely tender.

When the squash is soft, scoop out the flesh, stir it into the soup, and simmer for another 10 to 15 minutes.

Drain the veggies, reserving the liquid. Transfer the veggies to a food processor or blender and puree them, adding stock as needed. Whisk the puree back into the broth, stir in the lemon juice, and serve hot.

SPLIT PEA SOUP

If you add a bit of liquid smoke or diced tofu hot dogs to this soup, it will really remind you of the carnivorous version. When you're cooking a thick soup with legumes like split peas or lentils, it's a good idea to keep a really close eye on it. Because of their thickness, these soups burn easily. Cook them on lower heat than you would use for a brothy soup, and stir frequently.

1 pound split peas

8 cups Veggie Stock (page 74)

2 teaspoons sea salt

1 onion, chopped

3 cloves garlic, minced, or more to taste

2 carrots, chopped

2 red or Yukon gold potatoes (unpeeled), chopped

1 (6-ounce) can tomato sauce

1 tablespoon dry mustard or prepared mustard

1 tablespoon dried dill

Freshly ground black pepper

Sift through the split peas for rocks, then combine the split peas with the stock and salt in a soup pot. Bring to a boil, then lower the heat, and simmer gently for about 30 minutes, stirring occasionally. Stir in the onion, garlic, carrots, and potatoes and simmer gently for another 30 minutes, stirring often. Stir in the tomato sauce, mustard, and dill, and simmer gently for another 10 minutes, stirring frequently and adding more stock or water as needed if the soup gets too thick. Season with pepper to taste, and serve hot.

DAHL

MAKES 4 SERVINGS

This versatile soup can be used as a sauce for a rice dish or a curry, like Dev's Basic Curry (page 111). Of course, you can also eat it with a spoon. It's thick and satisfying, like split pea soup. You can substitute $2\frac{1}{2}$ teaspoons of curry powder for the cumin, coriander, turmeric, and cardamom if you wish.

4 cups water

1 cup red lentils or yellow split peas

2 cloves garlic, minced

1 tablespoon grated ginger

1 teaspoon ground cumin

$\frac{1}{2}$ teaspoon ground coriander

$\frac{1}{2}$ teaspoon ground turmeric

$\frac{1}{2}$ teaspoon ground cardamom

1 teaspoon sea salt

2 tablespoons freshly squeezed lemon juice (optional)

Sift through the lentils or split peas for rocks. Bring the water to a boil in a large saucepan. Stir in the lentils, garlic, ginger, cumin, coriander, turmeric, cardamom, and salt, then lower the heat, cover, and simmer gently for about 45 minutes, until the lentils are tender and beginning to break down. Stir frequently toward the end of the cooking time, and add more stock or water as needed if the dahl gets too thick. Stir in the lemon juice and serve hot.

BLACK-EYED PEA DAHL

MAKES 6 SERVINGS

In addition to eating this dahl with a spoon as a soup, you can also use it as a sauce on Spring Veggie Curry (page 113). You can substitute 1½ tablespoons of curry powder for the cumin, coriander, turmeric, and cardamom if you wish.

6 cups water

2 cups black-eyed peas

2 cloves garlic, minced

1 tablespoon grated ginger

2 teaspoons ground cumin

1 teaspoon ground coriander

1 teaspoon ground turmeric

½ teaspoon ground cardamom

1 teaspoon sea salt

Cayenne

Bring the water to a boil in a saucepan over high heat. Stir in the black-eyed peas, garlic, ginger, cumin, coriander, turmeric, cardamom, and salt, then lower the heat, cover, and simmer for about 1 hour, until the black-eyed peas start to break down. Season to taste with cayenne and serve hot.

GREEK LENTIL SOUP

MAKES 6 SERVINGS

As far as I'm concerned, you can't make too many different kinds of lentil soup. I enjoy this one with Greek Lasagna (page 106) or Spanakopita (page 131).

6 cups Veggie Stock (page 74) or water

2 cups lentils

1 onion, chopped

3 cloves garlic, minced

½ teaspoon ground cinnamon

1 teaspoon sea salt

2 carrots, chopped

1 tomato, chopped

2 tablespoons freshly squeezed lemon juice

Sift through the lentils for rocks. Combine the stock, lentils, onion, garlic, cinnamon, and salt in a soup pot and bring to a boil. Lower the heat, cover, and simmer gently for about 20 minutes. Stir in the carrots and tomato, cover, and simmer gently for another 20 to 30 minutes, until the veggies are soft and the lentils break down. Stir frequently toward the end of the cooking time, and add more stock or water as needed if the soup gets too thick. Stir in the lemon juice and serve hot.

EGYPTIAN LENTIL SOUP

MAKES 6 SERVINGS

Serve this soup with Dolmades (page 18). The mint gives it a lighter flavor than most lentil soups. You can add chopped kale, Swiss chard, or spinach if you like, or substitute any of those greens for the mustard greens. Use the stems from the greens or not, depending on your preference (see Pantry, page 210).

8 cups Veggie Stock (page 74) or water

2 teaspoons sea salt

2 cups lentils

2 tomatoes, chopped

2 carrots, chopped

1 onion, chopped

2 cloves garlic, minced

1 teaspoon ground cumin

1 teaspoon dried spearmint

1 bunch mustard greens, chopped

1 tablespoon freshly squeezed lemon juice

Combine the stock, salt, lentils, tomatoes, carrots, onion, garlic, cumin, and spearmint in a soup pot over high heat and bring to a boil. Lower the heat and simmer gently, uncovered, for 30 to 40 minutes. Stir in the mustard greens and simmer gently for another 20 minutes, until the greens are soft and the lentils break down. Stir often toward the end of the cooking time, and add stock or water as needed if the soup gets too thick. Stir in the lemon juice and serve hot.

BORSCHT

This soup has an amazing color; plus, it's high in iron. You can substitute dried dill for the fresh dill, but then it won't taste or smell like Grandmother's borscht.

6 beets

4 cups Veggie Stock (page 74) or water

2 parsnips, cut in chunks

2 carrots, cut in chunks

1 unpeeled potato, quartered

1 cup shredded cabbage

1 onion, quartered

2 cloves garlic

1 bunch fresh dill, coarsely chopped

1 teaspoon sea salt

$1/2$ teaspoon freshly ground black pepper

2 tablespoons white vinegar

Trim the tops off the beets, put the beets in a saucepan with enough water to cover by an inch or two, and boil for about 45 minutes.

Meanwhile, combine the stock, parsnips, carrots, potato, cabbage, onion, garlic, dill, salt, and pepper in a soup pot and bring to a boil. Lower the heat to medium and cook for about 45 minutes, until the vegetables are tender.

Using tongs, take a beet out of the pot, run cold water on it, and see if you can rub off the skin with your fingers. If you can, drain the beets and, as soon as they're cool enough to handle, peel them this way. If you can't, put the beet back in and continue cooking.

Once the beets are peeled and the other veggies are soft, drain the veggies in the soup pot, reserving the liquid. Transfer all of the cooked veggies (including the beets) to a food processor or blender and puree until smooth. You may need to puree in batches, adding more stock or water as needed for processing. Whisk the puree back into the broth, stir in the vinegar, and serve hot.

MUSHROOM-BARLEY SOUP

MAKES 4 SERVINGS

The seasonings in this hearty soup take me back to the Russian-Polish-Jewish food of my ancestors.

4 cups Veggie Stock (page 74) or water

1/2 cup pearled barley

8 ounces mushrooms, sliced

3 carrots, sliced

2 parsnips, peeled and sliced

1 onion, chopped

2 cloves garlic, minced

1 tablespoon dried dill

1 teaspoon sea salt

1/2 teaspoon freshly ground black pepper

Bring the stock to a boil in a soup pot, then stir in the barley, mushrooms, carrots, parsnips, onion, garlic, dill, salt, and pepper, lower the heat, cover, and simmer for 45 minutes to 1 hour, until the barley is soft and all of the vegetables are tender. Taste and add more salt if you like. Serve hot.

POTATO LEEK SOUP

Here's a simple, low-fat version of a tasty, traditional soup. Use any kind of potatoes except russets. Yukon golds make an especially creamy soup.

6 cups Veggie Stock (page 74) or water

4 potatoes (unpeeled), quartered

3 leeks, halved lengthwise, cleaned, and cut in chunks

2 cloves garlic, minced

2 tablespoons chopped parsley

1 teaspoon dried dill

1 teaspoon sea salt

$1/2$ teaspoon freshly ground black pepper

1 tablespoon freshly squeezed lemon juice (optional)

Bring the stock to a boil in a soup pot, then stir in the potatoes, leeks, garlic, parsley, dill, salt, and pepper. Lower the heat, cover, and simmer for 30 to 40 minutes, until the potatoes are soft.

Drain the veggies, reserving the liquid. Transfer the veggies to a food processor or blender and puree them, adding broth as needed, then whisk the puree back into the broth. Stir in the lemon juice and serve hot.

POTATO CORN CHOWDER

Mashing the potatoes makes this soup creamy, not unlike traditional dairy-based chowders. You can make an especially colorful soup by using an assortment of red, white, and even blue potatoes. Just make sure to stay away from russet potatoes for this recipe because they become mealy when you boil them.

6 cups Veggie Stock (page 74) or water

2 pounds potatoes (unpeeled), chopped

1 tomato, chopped

1 onion, chopped

2 cloves garlic, minced

1 teaspoon dried basil

1 teaspoon dried marjoram

1 teaspoon dried thyme

1 teaspoon sea salt

$1/2$ teaspoon freshly ground black pepper

1 cup frozen corn kernels

Combine the stock, potatoes, tomato, onion, garlic, basil, marjoram, thyme, salt, and pepper in a soup pot and bring to a boil. Lower the heat to medium and cook, stirring occasionally, for 30 to 40 minutes, until the potatoes are tender.

Using tongs or a slotted spoon, remove about 2 cups of the cooked potatoes, mash them with a potato masher or a fork, then return them to the soup and mix until somewhat smooth. Add the corn, stir until everything is thoroughly combined, and cook for another 5 to 10 minutes. Serve hot.

MAIN DISHES

LO MEIN

This is a colorful dish of veggies and noodles. The water chestnuts make it crunchy, and the soy sauce and toasted sesame oil give it a distinctive Chinese flavor. You can find rice wine for cooking in Asian groceries, or in the Asian food section of many mainstream groceries.

1 pound Asian noodles or spaghetti (see Pantry, page 208)

1½ tablespoons olive oil

1 onion, diced

2 cloves garlic, minced

2 tablespoons grated ginger

3 carrots, sliced

2 zucchini, sliced

1 baby bok choy, shredded

3 tablespoons soy sauce, or more to taste

2 tablespoons rice wine

1 tablespoon toasted sesame oil

1 (6-ounce) can sliced water chestnuts, drained

Bring a pot of salted water to a boil over medium-high heat, add the noodles, and cook, stirring often, for 8 to 10 minutes, until al dente. Drain the noodles well.

Meanwhile, heat the olive oil in a wok or large skillet over medium-low heat, add the onion, garlic, and ginger, and sauté for about 5 minutes, until the onion is soft. Add the carrots, sauté for another 3 to 5 minutes, then add the zucchini and bok choy and sauté for another 3 to 5 minutes, until the vegetables are tender. Stir in the soy sauce, rice wine, sesame oil, and water chestnuts, and cook for a few minutes longer, until everything is heated through.

Remove the veggies from the wok with a slotted spoon and set them aside, leaving the sauce in the pan. Turn the heat down to low and add the noodles to the wok, tossing them with tongs or chopsticks for about 2 minutes, until they absorb all of the liquid. Return the veggies to the wok, toss with the noodles, and serve.

YAKISOBA

This recipe shows off noodles and veggies, with traditional Japanese seasonings.

1 pound Asian noodles or spaghetti (see Pantry, page 208)

1 tablespoon olive oil

1 onion, chopped

2 cloves garlic, minced

2 tablespoons grated ginger

2 carrots, grated

1 small napa cabbage, shredded

3 tablespoons soy sauce

2 tablespoons rice vinegar

1 teaspoon raw sugar

Bring a pot of salted water to a boil over medium-high heat, add the noodles, and cook, stirring often, for 8 to 10 minutes, until al dente. Drain the noodles well.

Heat the oil in a wok or large skillet over medium-low heat, add the onion, garlic, and ginger, and sauté for about 5 minutes, until the onion is soft. Add the carrots and cabbage and sauté for another 5 minutes, until the cabbage is soft and reduced in size. Stir in the soy sauce, vinegar, and sugar, and cook for a minute longer.

Remove the veggies from the wok with a slotted spoon and set them aside, leaving the sauce. Turn the heat down to low and add the noodles, tossing them with tongs or chopsticks for 3 to 5 minutes, until they absorb all of the liquid. Return the veggies to the wok, toss with the noodles, and serve.

SOUTHEAST ASIAN GREENS AND NOODLES

MAKES 6 SERVINGS

Mint, basil, and lime juice make a light and refreshing sauce for this noodle dish. You can use the stems from the greens or not, depending on your preference (see Pantry, page 210). Serve with Southeast Asian Hot-and-Sour Soup with Lemongrass (page 82).

1 pound Asian noodles or spaghetti (see Pantry, page 208)

1 tablespoon olive oil

1 onion, chopped

2 cloves garlic, minced

1 tablespoon grated ginger

1 bunch collard greens, chopped

1 bunch mustard greens, chopped

1 bunch spinach, cleaned and stemmed

1 cup chopped bok choy

1 cup tightly packed Thai basil leaves (see Pantry, page 208)

$\frac{1}{2}$ cup tightly packed mint leaves

3 tablespoons soy sauce, or more to taste

2 tablespoons freshly squeezed lime juice, or more to taste

Bring a pot of salted water to a boil over medium-high heat, add the noodles, and cook, stirring often, for 8 to 10 minutes, until al dente. Drain the noodles well.

Meanwhile, heat the oil in a wok or large skillet over medium-low heat, add the onion, garlic, and ginger, and sauté for about 5 minutes, until the onion is soft. Add the collard greens and sauté for about 5 minutes, until they're wilted. Add the mustard greens, spinach, bok choy, basil, mint, and soy sauce and continue sautéing for another 5 to 10 minutes, until the greens are soft. Add the noodles and lime juice and toss with tongs, mixing until the noodles have soaked up all of the liquid. Serve hot.

PAD THAI

I think pad thai is one of the world's great dishes. The purple cabbage, orange carrots, and chopped peanuts make a gorgeous presentation atop the mound of elegantly flavored noodles. When shopping for the noodles, try to find the rice noodles from Thailand—they work best in this recipe. If you pick them up at an Asian market, you may be able to find the tamarind concentrate there, as well. If not, look for it at an Indian market or possibly a natural food store.

1 pound wide rice noodles

1 tablespoon olive oil

2 cloves garlic, minced

2 tablespoons tomato paste

1 tablespoon tamarind concentrate

1 tablespoon freshly squeezed lime juice

3 tablespoons soy sauce

1 teaspoon raw sugar

4 ounces firm tofu, cut in strips

2 carrots, grated

2 cups shredded red cabbage

1 cup bean sprouts

3 green onions, chopped

1/2 cup chopped roasted peanuts

Put the noodles in a bowl, pour in boiling water to cover by a couple of inches, and soak the noodles for 2 to 3 minutes, until they're soft. Drain the noodles well,

Meanwhile, heat the oil in a small saucepan over medium-low heat, add the garlic, and sauté for a minute or two. Add the tomato paste, tamarind concentrate, lime juice, soy sauce, and sugar and stir until the sugar dissolves and the sauce is smooth. Add the tofu and stir gently until it's evenly coated.

Put the noodles in a serving bowl, then pour in the sauce and tofu mixture and toss together with tongs. Top with the carrots, cabbage, sprouts, green onions, and peanuts and serve right away.

INDONESIAN NUTS AND NOODLES

MAKES 6 SERVINGS

Indonesian food typically uses quite a bit of fish, but it also relies heavily on nuts, which star in this vegetarian adaptation of a traditional dish.

1 pound Asian noodles or spaghetti (see Pantry, page 208)

$1/2$ cup roasted cashews

$1/2$ cup roasted peanuts

$1/2$ cup roasted hazelnuts

1 tablespoon olive oil

1 onion, chopped

2 cloves garlic, minced

$1^1/2$ tablespoons grated ginger

1 cup bean sprouts

3 tablespoons soy sauce

1 tablespoon molasses

1 tablespoon toasted sesame oil

Bring a pot of salted water to a boil over medium-high heat, add the noodles, and cook, stirring often, for 8 to 10 minutes, until al dente. Drain the noodles well.

Meanwhile, put the nuts in a food processor and pulse a few times to coarsely chop. Heat the olive oil in a wok or large skillet over medium-low heat, add the onion, garlic, and ginger, and sauté for 3 to 5 minutes, until the onion starts to soften. Stir in the nuts, sprouts, soy sauce, molasses, and sesame oil and cook for another few minutes, until the mixture is heated through. Add the noodles and toss everything with tongs or chopsticks for about 2 minutes, until the noodles absorb all of the liquid. Serve hot.

STUFFED SHELLS

MAKES 6 TO 8 SERVINGS

The sauce, tofu-spinach filling, and faux cheese give this dish the look and fool of a traditional Italian casserole. Although I tend to put the shells in a large casserole pan in one layer, you can also use a smaller, deeper pan and stack the shells, putting a layer of sauce between them.

1 pound large pasta shells

1 pound soft tofu

1 tablespoon olive oil

1 teaspoon sea salt

1 pound frozen spinach, thawed

4 cups Tomato Sauce (page 24)

1 cup Faux Cheese (page 40)

Preheat the oven to 350°F.

Bring a pot of salted water to a boil over medium-high heat, add the shells, and cook, stirring gently on occasion, for 8 to 10 minutes, until softened but not thoroughly cooked. Drain and rinse them in cold water.

Meanwhile, crumble the tofu, put it in a food processor with the oil and salt, then process until mostly smooth. Transfer the tofu to a bowl and stir in the spinach.

Pour a thin layer of the tomato sauce into a large casserole pan. Stuff each of the shells with a tablespoon or two of the tofu mixture, then arrange them on top of the sauce with the openings facing down. Spoon the remaining sauce over the shells and top with the "cheese." Cover and bake for 15 minutes, then remove the lid and bake 10 minutes longer, until the "cheese" starts to brown.

GREEK LASAGNA

The Greek seasonings in this casserole make for a lively twist on traditional lasagna. This recipe is familiar enough and yet different enough to surprise and delight people.

1 tablespoon olive oil

1 onion, chopped

5 cloves garlic, minced

1 small fennel bulb, cored and finely chopped

2 tablespoons chopped dill or 1 tablespoon dried

1$\frac{1}{2}$ teaspoons sea salt

$\frac{1}{2}$ teaspoon freshly ground black pepper

1 (28-ounce) can crushed tomatoes

2 tablespoons freshly squeezed lemon juice

12 to 15 spinach lasagna noodles

1 pound soft tofu

1 pound frozen spinach, thawed

$\frac{1}{2}$ cup chopped raw walnuts

$\frac{1}{2}$ cup pitted kalamata olives, finely chopped

1 cup Faux Cheese (page 40)

Heat the oil in a saucepan over medium-low heat, add the onion and garlic, and sauté for about 5 minutes, until the onion is soft. Add the fennel, dill, 1 teaspoon of the salt, and the pepper, and sauté for another 3 to 5 minutes. Stir in the tomatoes and simmer, stirring occasionally, for 10 minutes, then remove from the heat and stir in the lemon juice.

Meanwhile, bring a large pot of salted water to a boil over medium-high heat, add the lasagna noodles, and cook, stirring gently on occasion, for 8 to 10 minutes, until tender. Drain the noodles well.

Preheat the oven to 375°F. Crumble the tofu or puree it in a food processor, then stir in the spinach, walnuts, olives, and the remaining 1/2 teaspoon salt.

Spread a thin layer of the sauce in a casserole pan, then layer the ingredients as follows: one-third of the noodles, half of the tofu mixture, one-third of the sauce, another one-third of the noodles, the remaining tofu mixture, another one-third of the sauce, the rest of the noodles, the rest of the sauce, and all of the "cheese."

Cover and bake for 15 minutes, then uncover and bake another 10 minutes, until the "cheese" starts to brown. Serve hot.

PESTO LASAGNA

You can never have too many different kinds of lasagna! This one has a rich pesto filling.

12 to 15 lasagna noodles

2 pounds soft tofu

2 cups Pesto (page 27)

4 cups Tomato Sauce (page 24)

1 cup Faux Cheese (page 40)

Preheat the oven to 350°F.

Bring a large pot of salted water to a boil over medium-high heat, add the lasagna noodles, and cook, stirring gently on occasion, for 8 to 10 minutes, until al dente. Drain the noodles well.

Meanwhile, crumble the tofu or puree it in a food processor, then stir in the pesto.

Layer the ingredients in a casserole pan as follows: one-third of the tomato sauce, one-third of the noodles, half of the tofu mixture, another one-third of the noodles, another one-third of the sauce, the rest of the tofu mixture, the rest of the noodles, the rest of the sauce, and all of the "cheese."

Bake, uncovered, for 30 minutes, until the "cheese" starts to brown. Serve hot.

PASTA WITH OLIVES, ARTICHOKES, AND SUN-DRIED TOMATOES

MAKES 6 SERVINGS

This is a lovely pasta dish with fragrant basil, crunchy almonds, and sensual artichokes. Tubular or spiral pasta works well in this recipe.

1 pound colorful pasta

10 to 12 sun-dried tomatoes

2 tablespoons olive oil

2 cloves garlic, minced

1 (14-ounce) can quartered artichoke hearts, drained

1/4 cup pitted kalamata olives, sliced in thirds

3 tablespoons chopped basil

3 tablespoons chopped almonds

1/4 cup white wine

1 teaspoon sea salt

1/2 teaspoon freshly ground black pepper

Bring a pot of salted water to a boil over medium-high heat, add the pasta, and cook, stirring often, for 8 to 10 minutes, until al dente. Drain the pasta well.

Meanwhile, soak the sun-dried tomatoes in boiling water for a few minutes, until softened. Heat the oil in a large saucepan over low heat, add the garlic, and sauté for 3 to 4 minutes, until soft. Drain the tomatoes and, when they're cool enough to handle, finely chop them. Stir the tomatoes into the garlic, along with the artichoke hearts, olives, basil, almonds, wine, salt, and pepper. Cook, stirring occasionally, for another 5 to 10 minutes, until heated through. Add the pasta, mix well, and serve hot.

PASTA PRIMAVERA

MAKES 6 SERVINGS

Make this dish in early spring. It uses those fresh herbs and tender veggies that have been in short supply through the long winter. Tubular or spiral pasta works especially well in this recipe.

1 pound colorful pasta

1 tablespoon olive oil

1 red onion, chopped

2 cloves garlic, minced

1 bunch asparagus, cut in bite-sized pieces

1 red bell pepper, cut in strips

1 cup sugar snap peas, trimmed

1 bunch Swiss chard, chopped

½ cup white wine

3 tablespoons chopped basil

1 teaspoon sea salt

Bring a pot of salted water to a boil over medium-high heat, add the pasta, and cook, stirring often, for 8 to 10 minutes, until al dente. Drain the pasta well.

Heat the oil in a large saucepan over medium-low heat, add the onion and garlic, and sauté for 5 minutes, until the onion is soft. Stir in the asparagus, bell pepper, peas, chard, wine, basil, and salt and cook, stirring occasionally, for 10 to 15 minutes, until the veggies are just soft. Add the pasta, mix well, and cook, stirring occasionally, for another 5 minutes, until heated through. Serve hot.

DEV'S BASIC CURRY

I call this my "basic" curry because it's simple and tasty, with everything it needs and nothing more. You can substitute 3½ teaspoons of curry powder for the cumin, coriander, turmeric, and cardamom. Serve with Pulao (page 192).

2 red potatoes (unpeeled), chopped

1 tablespoon olive oil

1 onion, diced

2 tablespoons minced garlic

2 tablespoons grated ginger

1 teaspoon ground cumin

1 teaspoon ground coriander

1 teaspoon ground turmeric

½ teaspoon ground cardamom

½ teaspoon anise or fennel seed (optional)

1 teaspoon sea salt

Pinch of cayenne (optional)

2 carrots, chopped

1 head cauliflower, broken into bite-sized pieces

2 cups broccoli florets

¼ cup Veggie Stock (page 74) or water

1 tomato, diced

1 (14-ounce) can chickpeas, drained and rinsed, or 2 cups cooked

2 tablespoons coconut milk

(continued)

Dev's Basic Curry, continued

Put the potatoes in a saucepan, add water to cover by an inch or two, and bring to a boil over high heat. Lower the heat to medium, cover, and cook for 8 to 10 minutes, until soft.

Meanwhile, heat the oil in a large saucepan over medium-low heat, add the onion, garlic, ginger, cumin, coriander, turmeric, cardamom, anise, salt, and cayenne, and sauté for 5 minutes, until the onion is soft. Stir in the carrots, cauliflower, broccoli, and stock and cook, stirring occasionally, for about 10 minutes, until the veggies are tender. Stir in the tomato and cook for another 3 minutes, then stir in the chickpeas, cooked potatoes, and coconut milk. Raise the heat to medium, cook for another 2 minutes, until heated through, and serve hot.

SPRING VEGGIE CURRY

Nothing says spring quite like asparagus. Here it stars in a curry dish, along with other spring favorites. You can substitute $3^1/_2$ teaspoons of curry powder for the cumin, coriander, turmeric, and cardamom. Serve with Pulao (page 192).

$1^1/_2$ tablespoons olive oil

1 onion, chopped

2 cloves garlic, minced

1 tablespoon grated ginger

1 teaspoon ground cumin

1 teaspoon ground coriander

1 teaspoon ground turmeric

$^1/_2$ teaspoon ground cardamom

1 teaspoon sea salt

1 bunch asparagus, cut in bite-sized pieces

1 bunch Swiss chard, chopped

8 ounces sugar snap peas, trimmed

1 tomato, chopped, or $^1/_2$ cup canned crushed tomatoes

1 red bell pepper, cut in bite-sized pieces

$^1/_4$ cup coconut milk

Heat the oil in a saucepan or skillet over medium-low heat, add the onion, garlic, ginger, cumin, coriander, turmeric, cardamom, and salt, and sauté for 5 minutes, until the onion is soft. Stir in the asparagus, chard, peas, tomato, and bell pepper and sauté for another 10 minutes, adding a bit of stock or water if it seems too dry. Stir in the coconut milk, cook for another minute, and serve hot.

YAM AND CHARD CURRY

MAKES 4 SERVINGS

This is a colorful and highly nutritious curry. Serve it with Pulao (page 192). You can substitute 3½ teaspoons of curry powder for the cumin, coriander, turmeric, and cardamom.

1 tablespoon olive oil

2 yams, peeled and cut in small pieces

2 leeks, cleaned and sliced ½ inch thick

1 tablespoon grated ginger

1 teaspoon ground cumin

1 teaspoon ground coriander

1 teaspoon turmeric

½ teaspoon ground cardamom

1 teaspoon sea salt

1 bunch Swiss chard (preferably red), chopped

¼ cup red wine

Cayenne

Heat the oil in a large saucepan over medium-low heat, then stir in the yams, leeks, ginger, cumin, coriander, turmeric, cardamom, and salt, cover, and cook for 10 to 15 minutes, until the yams are soft. Add a few tablespoons of water if the yams start to stick. Stir in the chard and wine, turn the heat down to low, cover, and cook for another 5 to 10 minutes, until the chard is completely wilted. Season to taste with cayenne and serve hot.

PEA AND POTATO CURRY

MAKES 4 TO 6 SERVINGS

This dish is simple and satisfying, and it also makes a great filling for samosas (East Indian turnovers). Serve with Tamarind Date Chutney (page 30) on the side. Don't use russet potatoes for this dish, as they'll crumble, whereas red or yellow potatoes will hold their shape. You can substitute 2½ teaspoons of curry powder for the cumin, coriander, turmeric, and cardamom.

4 red or yellow potatoes (unpeeled), chopped

1 tablespoon olive oil

1 onion, chopped

2 cloves garlic, minced

1 tablespoon grated ginger

1 teaspoon ground cumin

½ teaspoon ground coriander

½ teaspoon ground turmeric

½ teaspoon ground cardamom

1 teaspoon sea salt

1 tomato, chopped

⅓ cup frozen peas

Put the potatoes in a saucepan, add water to cover by an inch or two, and bring to a boil over high heat. Lower the heat to medium, cover, and cook for 8 to 10 minutes, until soft.

Meanwhile, heat the oil in a saucepan or skillet over medium-low heat, add the onion, garlic, ginger, cumin, coriander, turmeric, cardamom, and salt, and sauté for about 5 minutes, until the onion is soft. Stir in the tomato and cook, stirring occasionally, for about 5 minutes longer, until it breaks down. Stir in the peas and cook a few minutes longer, until heated through. Serve hot.

WINTER VEGGIE CURRY

MAKES 6 SERVINGS

This filling and satisfying curry features a rich variety of winter veggies. Serve with Pulao (page 192). You can substitute 3$\frac{1}{2}$ teaspoons of curry powder for the cumin, coriander, turmeric, and cardamom.

1$\frac{1}{2}$ tablespoons olive oil

2 leeks, sliced lengthwise, cleaned, and chopped

2 cloves garlic, minced

1 tablespoon grated ginger

1 teaspoon ground cumin

1 teaspoon ground coriander

1 teaspoon ground turmeric

$\frac{1}{2}$ teaspoon ground cardamom

1 teaspoon sea salt

2 parsnips, peeled and chopped

2 carrots, chopped

1 yam, peeled and cut in bite-sized chunks

1 bunch kale, chopped

$\frac{1}{2}$ cup Veggie Stock (page 74) or water

Cayenne

Heat the oil in a large saucepan or skillet over medium-low heat, add the leeks, garlic, ginger, cumin, coriander, turmeric, cardamom, and salt, and sauté for 3 to 5 minutes, until the leeks are tender. Stir in the parsnips, carrots, yam, kale, and stock, cover, and cook for about 10 to 15 minutes, until the yams and parsnips are soft. Season to taste with cayenne and serve hot.

PALAK TOFU

MAKES 6 SERVINGS

You may be familiar with the popular Indian dish *palak paneer*. In this version, I've substituted tofu for the *paneer*, a fresh cheese commonly used in Indian cookery. You can substitute 2½ teaspoons of curry powder for the cumin, coriander, turmeric, and cardamom. Serve with Pulao (page 192).

1½ tablespoons olive oil

1 onion, chopped

2 cloves garlic, minced

1 tablespoon grated ginger

1 teaspoon ground cumin

½ teaspoon ground coriander

½ teaspoon ground turmeric

½ teaspoon ground cardamom

1 teaspoon sea salt

1 (10-ounce) package frozen spinach, thawed

8 ounces firm or extra firm tofu, cubed

1 tomato, chopped

Cayenne

Heat the oil in a large saucepan or skillet over medium-low heat, add the onion, garlic, ginger, cumin, coriander, turmeric, cardamom, and salt, and sauté about 5 minutes, until the onion is soft. Stir in the spinach and cook for a few minutes longer, until it's heated through, then add the tofu and tomato, mix gently, and cook, stirring often (and gently), for another 5 minutes, until heated through. Season to taste with cayenne and serve hot.

TAMALES

MAKES ENOUGH FOR 15 TAMALES

Once a gift tied in corn husk wrappers that the Aztecs offered to their gods, over time tamales became a traditional preparation for family feasts and holidays. Wrappers vary from region to region. North of the border, we're most familiar with tamales wrapped in corn husks, but they can also be wrapped in banana leaves or avocado leaves. The dough, made from ground corn mixed with limewater, can be made with either fresh corn or masa harina, an instant cornmeal mixture. Lard is the traditional shortening used in the dough, as it makes the tamales especially light and fluffy, but you can also get good results with vegetable oil.

15 corn husks

2 cups water

1 teaspoon sea salt

1 tablespoon canola oil, corn oil, or olive oil

2 cups masa harina

Soak the husks in hot water. Prepare the filling of your choice (see pages 119–121).

Combine the 2 cups water, salt, and oil in a saucepan over high heat and bring to a boil. Turn off the heat, slowly add the masa, and stir until it forms a smooth dough. When the masa mixture is cool enough to handle, roll it into $2\frac{1}{2}$–inch diameter balls. Wet your hands as needed to prevent sticking.

Lay down a corn husk with a narrow end closest to you and place a ball of masa in the center. Flatten the ball, then lay a spoonful of filling in the middle. Fold the upper corners of the husk in so they meet in the center. This should close the flattened masa around the filling. Using the husk, press the edges of the dough together.

Unfold the husk, then fold the bottom up and roll from left to right to close the tamale. If the husk isn't big enough to hold the tamale closed, tie a piece of string or a strip of husk around it. Repeat with the remaining husks, masa, and filling.

Cook the tamales in a vegetable steamer for 15 minutes, until the masa is soft and they're heated through.

SQUASH AND OLIVE FILLING

MAKES ENOUGH FOR 15 TAMALES

1 acorn squash

1/2 cup raw almonds, chopped

1/2 cup sliced black olives

2 tablespoons red wine vinegar

1 teaspoon chili powder, mild or hot

1/2 teaspoon ground cumin

1/2 teaspoon dried oregano

1 teaspoon sea salt

Cut the squash in half, scoop out the seeds, and cut the squash into pieces that will fit in your steamer. Steam for 30 to 40 minutes, until it's very soft. Scoop out the pulp and mix all of the ingredients together.

BEAN AND CHIPOTLE FILLING

MAKES ENOUGH FOR 15 TAMALES

8 sun-dried tomatoes

2 cups cooked kidney, pinto, or black beans, or 1 (15-ounce) can, drained and rinsed

3 canned chipotle peppers in adobo, with their sauce, finely chopped

2 tablespoons red wine vinegar

$\frac{1}{2}$ teaspoon sea salt

Soak the sun-dried tomatoes in boiling water for a few minutes, until softened. Drain them and, when they're cool enough to handle, chop them finely. Mix all of the ingredients together.

CHILE, TOMATO, AND CORN FILLING

MAKES ENOUGH FOR 15 TAMALES

1 tomato, chopped in $\frac{1}{2}$–inch pieces

1 (4-ounce) can diced mild green chiles

1 cup frozen corn kernels

2 tablespoons red wine vinegar

$\frac{1}{2}$ teaspoon sea salt

Mix all of the ingredients together.

ASPARAGUS AND POBLANO FILLING

MAKES ENOUGH FOR 15 TAMALES

1 tablespoon olive oil

1 pound asparagus, chopped in $1/2$-inch pieces

1 poblano chile, finely chopped

$1/2$ teaspoon chili powder, mild or hot

$1/4$ teaspoon ground cumin

$1/4$ teaspoon dried oregano

$1/4$ teaspoon sea salt

Heat the oil in a saucepan over medium-low heat, add the asparagus, chile, chili powder, cumin, oregano, and salt, and sauté for about 5 minutes, until the veggies are soft.

SPINACH AND PUMPKIN SEED FILLING

MAKES ENOUGH FOR 15 TAMALES

1 (10-ounce) package frozen spinach, thawed

$1/2$ cup toasted pumpkin seeds

3 tablespoons chopped cilantro

$1 1/2$ tablespoons freshly squeezed lime juice

$1/2$ teaspoon sea salt

Mix together all of the ingredients.

TAMALE PIE

With this recipe you get the great stone-ground corn flavor of tamales without the somewhat time-consuming work of individually assembling them.

10 to 12 sun-dried tomatoes

2 cups water

2 teaspoons sea salt

1 tablespoon olive oil

2 cups masa harina or masa mixta

2 canned chipotle peppers in adobo, with their sauce, finely chopped

2 cups cooked black or pinto beans, or 1 (15-ounce) can, drained and rinsed

1 tablespoon red wine vinegar

1 cup Red Chile Salsa (page 38)

1 cup Faux Cheese (page 40)

Preheat the oven to 375°F. Soak the sun-dried tomatoes in boiling water for a few minutes, until softened. Combine the 2 cups water, 1 teaspoon of the salt, and the oil in a saucepan over high heat and bring to a boil. Turn off the heat, add the masa, and stir until smooth. Spoon half of this mixture into a medium casserole pan, then spread it over the bottom and up the sides.

Drain the sun-dried tomatoes and, when they're cool enough to handle, chop them finely. Put the tomatoes in a bowl and stir in the chipotles, beans, vinegar, and the remaining teaspoon of salt.

Pour the bean mixture into the masa shell in the casserole pan. Flatten handfuls of the remaining masa dough into patties and arrange them over the beans. It's okay to leave gaps. Spread the salsa over the top, then the "cheese."

Bake for 20 to 30 minutes, until the top starts to brown. Serve hot.

VEGGIE QUESADILLAS

MAKES 6 SERVINGS

Quesadillas are the signature dish at my restaurant, and this is the vegan version we offer. You can use whatever veggies are in season, as we do. This recipe offers a midsummer selection. If you can find tomato or spinach tortillas, their color will add eye appeal. Cut the quesadillas with a pizza cutter if you have one.

1 tablespoon plus 1 teaspoon olive oil

1 yellow or red onion, halved lengthwise then cut in semicircles

2 zucchini, finely chopped

2 cups loosely packed chopped red Swiss chard

1 cup chopped green or red cabbage

1 teaspoon chili powder, mild or hot

$1/2$ teaspoon ground cumin

$1/2$ teaspoon dried oregano

1 teaspoon sea salt

6 (10-inch) flour tortillas

1 cup Faux Cheese (page 40)

Heat the 1 tablespoon of olive oil in a large skillet over medium-high heat, add the onion, zucchini, chard, cabbage, chili powder, cumin, oregano, and salt, and sauté for 5 to 10 minutes, until the veggies are soft. Remove the veggies from the pan, then rinse it and dry it.

To assemble the quesadillas, spread one-sixth of the "cheese" on each tortilla, then cover half of the surface with one-sixth of the veggies. Fold each quesadilla in half to form a semicircle.

Heat the 1 teaspoon of olive oil in the skillet over medium-low heat, and spread it evenly over the surface of the pan. Cook the quesadillas one or two at a time for about 1 minute on each side, until they just start to brown. Cut each quesadilla into 4 wedges.

ENCHILADA PIE

This dish is easier than traditional enchiladas because no rolling is involved, and it's just as delicious.

1 tablespoon olive oil

1 onion, chopped

2 cloves garlic, minced

1 Anaheim chile, diced, or 2 tablespoons canned diced mild green chiles

1 tablespoon chili powder, mild or hot

1 teaspoon dried oregano

1 teaspoon ground cumin

1 teaspoon sea salt

1 zucchini, chopped

1 green bell pepper, chopped

3 cups cooked pinto beans, or $1^{1}/_{2}$ (15-ounce) cans, drained

$^{1}/_{2}$ cup frozen corn kernels

Hot sauce

1 cup Red Chile Salsa (page 38)

18 corn tortillas

2 cups Faux Cheese (page 40)

Preheat the oven to 375°F.

Heat the oil in a saucepan over medium-low heat, add the onion, garlic, chile, chili powder, oregano, cumin, and salt, and sauté for a minute, then add the zucchini and bell pepper and sauté for another 5 to 10 minutes, until the veggies are soft. Add the beans and corn and mix well, mashing the beans a bit. Season to taste with hot sauce.

Spread a layer of the salsa in a large casserole pan, then arrange 6 of the tortillas to cover it. Spoon half the bean mixture over the tortillas, then arrange another 6 tortillas atop the beans. Cover with a layer of salsa and then the rest of the beans. Arrange the remaining 6 tortillas over the beans, then spread the remaining salsa and all of the "cheese" over the top.

Bake for 20 to 30 minutes, until the top starts to brown. Serve hot.

SKEWERED VEGGIES IN THAI BARBECUE SAUCE

MAKES 10 TO 12 SKEWERS

Roasting and grilling draw out the finest flavor in vegetables. This dish uses these techniques to concentrate and caramelize the complex, refreshing flavors typical of Southeast Asian cuisine. Serve this recipe with Pad Thai (page 102) or Spinach and Tofu in Peanut Sauce (page 148). You'll need 10 to 12 wooden skewers.

MARINADE

1 cup tomato juice

2 tablespoons soy sauce

1 tablespoon freshly squeezed lime juice

1 tablespoon coconut milk (optional)

1 tablespoon chopped Thai basil (see Pantry, page 208)

1 teaspoon grated ginger

VEGGIES

1 zucchini, chopped

10 small mushrooms

1 green bell pepper, cut in strips

1 red bell pepper, cut in strips

1 cup broccoli florets

1 cup cauliflower florets

1 red onion, quartered and separated into layers

Preheat the oven to 400°F, or if you're going to grill on an open flame, prepare a medium-hot grill. For grilling, soak the skewers in water while you prepare the veggies.

To prepare the marinade, put all of the ingredients in a shallow bowl or dish and stir until thoroughly combined. Marinate the veggies in the sauce, ideally for at least 30 minutes.

Skewer the veggies, putting a variety of veggies on each skewer and paying attention to the arrangement of the colors. Roast the skewers on a baking pan for 20 minutes, until they start to brown. Alternatively, grill them for about 2 minutes, then turn them and grill them for two more minutes.

INDONESIAN STIR-FRY

Tempeh is a fermented soybean product first developed in Indonesia. It's denser than tofu, and because it's fermented it's easier to digest. Soy sauce, molasses, and toasted sesame oil make a sweet, musky sauce for this dish. Serve over rice.

1 tablespoon olive oil

8 ounces tempeh, cubed

1 onion, diced

2 cloves garlic, minced

1 tablespoon grated ginger

2 carrots, chopped

2 tablespoons soy sauce

1 baby bok choy, chopped

1 cup bean sprouts

1/4 cup chopped hazelnuts

1 tablespoon molasses

1 teaspoon toasted sesame oil

Heat the olive oil in a wok or large skillet over medium heat, add the tempeh, and cook, turning the tempeh a few times, for about 3 minutes, until browned. Add the onion, garlic, and ginger, turn the heat down to medium-low, and sauté for about 5 minutes, until the onion is soft. Add the carrots and soy sauce and sauté for another 5 minutes, then add the bok choy, sauté a few minutes longer, then stir in the sprouts, hazelnuts, molasses, and sesame oil and cook a few minutes longer, until heated through. Serve right away.

CHINESE VEGGIES IN BLACK BEAN SAUCE

MAKES 4 TO 6 SERVINGS

Chinese food is characterized by a subtle interplay of colors, flavors, and textures. This mixed vegetable dish has a sweet, sour, salty sauce and a plentiful array of vegetables. The Black Bean Sauce is less salty than most commercial versions, believe it or not. Salted, fermented black beans are available at some Asian markets, and brown rice syrup is available in natural food stores. Serve with Fried Rice (page 190).

BLACK BEAN SAUCE

1 (8-ounce) package salted black beans, rinsed and checked for stones

2 cloves garlic, minced

2 tablespoons grated ginger

1 cup water

2 tablespoons rice vinegar

1 tablespoon toasted sesame oil

1 tablespoon brown rice syrup

VEGGIE MIXTURE

2 tablespoons olive oil

1 onion, chopped

2 cloves garlic, chopped

1 tablespoon grated ginger

2 carrots, chopped

2 zucchini, chopped

1 cup chopped green beans

1 small bok choy, shredded

10 mushrooms, chopped

1 green or red bell pepper, chopped

1 cup bean sprouts

1 (5-ounce) can sliced water chestnuts, drained

1 (5-ounce) can sliced bamboo shoots, drained

To make the sauce, combine all the ingredients in a food processor or blender and process until smooth. Set aside.

To make the vegetable mixture, heat the oil in a wok or skillet over medium-low heat, add the onion, garlic, and ginger, and sauté for about 5 minutes, until the onion is soft. Add the carrots and sauté another 3 to 5 minutes, then add the zucchini, green beans, bok choy, mushrooms, bell pepper, and sprouts and sauté another 8 to 10 minutes, until the veggies are tender. Sprinkle in a few tablespoons of water if the mixture seems too dry. Stir in the water chestnuts, bamboo shoots, and the sauce and cook, stirring occasionally, another 5 minutes, until heated through. Serve hot.

KEDGEREE

MAKES 6 SERVINGS

I've adapted this Middle Eastern staple of lentils and rice by adding a variety of veggies for color and texture. Serve this dish along with Hummus (page 2), Baba Ghanoush (page 6), and pita bread.

6 cups water

1 cup brown rice

1 cup lentils

2 tablespoons olive oil

1 onion, chopped

3 cloves garlic, minced

3 carrots, chopped

6 to 8 mushrooms, quartered

1 bunch kale, chopped

1 teaspoon ground cumin

1 teaspoon dry mustard

1 teaspoon sea salt

1 tablespoon freshly squeezed lemon juice, or more to taste

Bring 2 cups of the water to a boil in a small saucepan over high heat, then stir in the rice, lower the heat, cover, and simmer for about 45 minutes, until all of the liquid is absorbed. In a separate saucepan, bring the remaining 4 cups of water to a boil over high heat, stir in the lentils, then lower the heat, cover, and simmer for 40 to 50 minutes, until soft. Drain the lentils.

Meanwhile, heat the oil in a skillet over medium-low heat, add the onion and garlic, and sauté for about 5 minutes, until the onion is soft. Add the carrots, mushrooms, kale, cumin, mustard, and salt, and sauté for another 5 minutes, until the veggies are tender. Add the lentils, rice, and lemon juice and cook and stir until everything is thoroughly combined and heated through. Serve hot.

SPANAKOPITA

MAKES 12 SERVINGS

This unusual take on spanakopita features crispy layers of phyllo dough stuffed with a tangy and hearty lentil filling. If you're using frozen phyllo, you need to defrost it a day before you use it (see Pantry, page 213), so plan ahead. Also, a pastry brush will come in very handy here.

1 package phyllo dough

1 cup olive oil

1 onion, chopped

4 cloves garlic, minced

1 (10-ounce) package frozen spinach, thawed

2 cups cooked lentils

2 tablespoons freshly squeezed lemon juice

1 pound soft tofu, crumbled

2 teaspoons sea salt

1 teaspoon dried dill

$1/2$ teaspoon anise seed (optional)

Set the phyllo out at room temperature while you prepare the other ingredients. Preheat the oven to 375°F.

Heat 1 tablespoon of the oil in a skillet over medium-low heat, add the onion and garlic, and sauté for 5 minutes, until the onion is soft. Stir in the spinach, lentils, lemon juice, tofu, salt, dill, and anise and remove from the heat. Drain any excess liquid before proceeding.

(continued)

Spanakopita, continued

Use a pastry brush to spread a layer of olive oil on an 11 by 17-inch baking pan. Spread a sheet of phyllo on the baking pan, brush it with oil, and repeat with 11 more sheets. Don't agonize if some sheets rip or stick together. The final product will look fine.

Spread the filling as evenly and gently as possible over the phyllo, then layer the remaining phyllo dough over the filling, brushing each sheet with oil as before. Score the spanakopita into thirds lengthwise and fourths crosswise to make 12 rectangles, cutting down just to the filling. Bake for about 30 minutes, until the top is golden brown. Cut all the way through and serve.

SPANISH VEGGIE STEW

This tomato-based stew is full of veggies and accented by the bold flavor of green olives. Serve it with Spanish Rice (page 191).

1 tablespoon olive oil

1 onion, chopped

2 cloves garlic, minced

1 teaspoon sea salt

2 carrots, chopped

1 zucchini, chopped

1 bunch kale, chopped

1 cup frozen peas

1 (28-ounce) can crushed tomatoes

1/4 cup sliced green olives

2 tablespoons chopped parsley

Heat the oil in a large saucepan over medium-low heat, add the onion, garlic, and salt, and sauté for about 5 minutes, until the onion is soft. Add the carrots and zucchini and sauté for another 5 to 10 minutes, until the carrots are soft. Stir in the kale, peas, tomatoes, olives, and parsley and cook, stirring occasionally, 10 to 15 minutes longer, until the kale is tender. Serve hot.

FALAFEL

MAKES 4 SANDWICHES

This is one of the world's great sandwiches. It is traditionally made without meat or dairy, so it doesn't require any adaptation to make a vegan version. It's generally deep-fried, but I prefer to pan-fry the patties because the process is less messy and uses less fat. If you like them deep-fried, you can roll them in a bit of flour and fry according to the instructions in the Basic Techniques section (page 219). Alternatively, you can brush the patties with a bit of oil and bake at 375°F for 10 to 15 minutes.

PATTIES

2 cups cooked chickpeas, or 1 (15-ounce) can, drained

2 tablespoons tahini, ideally the thicker stuff toward the bottom of the container

1 clove garlic, minced

2 teaspoons freshly squeezed lemon juice

1 tablespoon dried parsley

$1/2$ teaspoon sea salt

2 tablespoons olive oil

SANDWICH FIXINGS

4 pita pockets

4 leaves romaine lettuce, chopped

2 Roma tomatoes, finely chopped

$1/2$ cup Tahini Dressing (page 48)

To make the patties, combine the chickpeas, tahini, garlic, lemon juice, parsley, salt, and 1 tablespoon of the oil in a food processor and process until smooth.

Heat the remaining tablespoon of oil in a skillet over medium heat, then drop tablespoons of the chickpea mixture into the pan and form into patties by flattening them a bit with a spatula. Cook for 3 to 4 minutes, until the bottom is browned, then flip them over and cook the other side for about 3 to 4 minutes longer, again until browned.

To make the sandwiches, trim an inch or so off one side of each pita and open the pocket. Stuff it with a couple of patties, a handful of chopped lettuce and one-fourth of the tomato, then drizzle Tahini Dressing in over the filling. If you're using Greek pita, (see Pantry, page 213) you can just arrange the patties, veggies, and sauce in a row along the length of each pita, then wrap the bread around it to make a cone. Serve right away.

ACORN SQUASH RATATOUILLE

MAKES 6 SERVINGS

This hearty dish is a celebration of the flavors of late summer. Serve it over polenta.

1 acorn squash

2 tablespoons olive oil

1 onion, diced

2 cloves garlic, minced

1 eggplant, cubed

1 small fennel bulb, cored and finely chopped

1 tablespoon dried or 3 tablespoons chopped basil

1 teaspoon dried marjoram

1 teaspoon dried tarragon

$\frac{1}{2}$ teaspoon freshly ground black pepper

1 (28-ounce) can crushed tomatoes

1 teaspoon sea salt

Cut the squash in half, scoop out the seeds, and cut it into pieces that will fit in your steamer. Steam for 30 to 40 minutes, until very soft.

Meanwhile, heat the oil in a saucepan or skillet over medium-low heat, add the onion, garlic, eggplant, fennel, basil, marjoram, tarragon, and pepper, and sauté for about 15 minutes, until the eggplant is very soft. Stir in the tomatoes and salt, turn the heat down to low, and cook, stirring occasionally, for another 20 minutes. Scoop the squash pulp out of the skin, chop it coarsely, and stir it into the ratatouille. Cook a minute longer, until heated through, and serve hot.

EGGPLANT PARMESAN

MAKES 6 SERVINGS

This is a vegan version of the succulent Italian favorite. Steaming the eggplant is a low-fat alternative to the traditional practice of frying it. The pieces will be fragile after they're steamed and they may break apart as you assemble the dish, but they'll eventually be covered by the sauce and the "cheese," so the finished product will look fine. Serve with Antipasto Salad (page 68) and Tomato Herb Bread (page 22).

2 eggplants

1 pound soft tofu

1 tablespoon olive oil

$\frac{1}{2}$ teaspoon sea salt

1 pound frozen spinach, thawed

4 cups Tomato Sauce (page 24)

2 cups Faux Cheese (page 40)

Preheat the oven to 350°F.

Slice the eggplant $\frac{1}{4}$ inch thick and steam for 5 minutes, until tender.

Crumble the tofu into a bowl, then stir in the oil, salt, and spinach. Layer the ingredients in a casserole pan as follows: one-third of the tomato sauce, half the eggplant, another one-third of the sauce, all of the tofu mixture, the rest of the eggplant, the rest of the sauce, and all of the "cheese."

Cover and bake for 15 minutes, then remove the cover, and bake for another 10 minutes, until the "cheese" starts to brown.

SESAME BAKED TOFU

MAKES 3 TO 4 SERVINGS

We always include a marinated tofu entrée on the menu at my restaurant, changing the flavor every week. We never run out of ideas. The selections that follow include many customer favorites. Serve baked tofu hot, as an entrée, or use cold or room-temperature slabs on sandwiches.

1/3 cup tahini

1/2 cup soy sauce

2 tablespoons nutritional yeast

2 tablespoons rice vinegar

1 pound firm tofu

Preheat the oven to 375°F. Oil a baking sheet.

Put the tahini, soy sauce, nutritional yeast, and vinegar in a shallow bowl and stir until thoroughly combined. Cut the tofu into slabs 1/4 inch thick. Dip each slab in the sauce, then arrange the tofu on the prepared baking sheet. Bake for 30 minutes, until it starts to brown.

CARIBBEAN BAKED TOFU

Serve this tofu dish with Caribbean Black-Eyed Pea Salad (page 67) for a great summer meal.

2 tablespoons water

2 tablespoons soy sauce

2 tablespoons coconut milk

1 tablespoon cider vinegar

$1/2$ teaspoon crushed red pepper (optional)

$1/2$ teaspoon thyme

$1/4$ teaspoon allspice

1 pound firm tofu

Preheat the oven to 375°F. Oil a baking sheet.

Put the water, soy sauce, coconut milk, vinegar, crushed red pepper, thyme, and allspice in a shallow bowl and stir until thoroughly combined. Cut the tofu into slabs $1/4$ inch thick. Dip each slab in the sauce, then arrange the tofu on the prepared baking sheet. Bake for 30 minutes, until it starts to brown.

VIETNAMESE BAKED TOFU

MAKES 4 SERVINGS

This baked tofu dish uses a medley of fresh herbs. Serve it with Southeast Asian Greens and Noodles (page 101).

3 tablespoons water

2 tablespoons soy sauce

Freshly squeezed juice of $1/2$ lime

1 tablespoon chopped mint

1 tablespoon chopped cilantro

1 tablespoon chopped Thai basil (see Pantry, page 208)

1 teaspoon grated ginger

1 pound firm tofu

Preheat the oven to 375°F. Oil a baking sheet.

Put the water, soy sauce, lime juice, mint, cilantro, basil, and ginger in a bowl and stir until thoroughly combined. Cut the tofu into slabs $1/4$ inch thick. Dip each slab in the sauce, then arrange the tofu on the prepared baking sheet. Bake for 30 minutes, until it starts to brown.

WASABI-TERIYAKI BAKED TOFU

For a quick, tasty, high-protein dinner, serve this tofu with brown rice and Miso-Noodle Soup (page 79).

3 tablespoons water

2 tablespoons soy sauce

1 tablespoon rice vinegar

$1/2$ teaspoon raw sugar

$1/2$ teaspoon wasabi powder

1 pound firm tofu

Preheat the oven to 375°F. Oil a baking sheet.

Put the water, soy sauce, vinegar, sugar, and wasabi powder in a shallow bowl and stir until the sugar is dissolved and everything is thoroughly combined. Cut the tofu into slabs $1/4$ inch thick. Dip each slab in the sauce, then arrange the tofu on the prepared baking sheet. Bake for 30 minutes, until it starts to brown.

HAWAIIAN BAKED TOFU

MAKES 4 SERVINGS

The liquid smoke in this recipe is reminiscent of the flavor of ham, which is so often used in traditional Hawaiian foods.

3 tablespoons canned crushed pineapple

2 tablespoons water

2 tablespoons soy sauce

1 tablespoon rice vinegar

$\frac{1}{2}$ teaspoon liquid smoke

1 pound firm tofu

Preheat the oven to 375°F. Oil a baking sheet.

Put the pineapple, water, soy sauce, vinegar, and liquid smoke in a bowl and stir until thoroughly combined. Cut the tofu into slabs $\frac{1}{4}$ inch thick. Dip each slab in the sauce, then arrange the tofu on the prepared baking sheet. Bake for 30 minutes, until it starts to brown.

COCONUT-LIME BAKED TOFU

MAKES 4 SERVINGS

I get a real satisfaction from creating wonderful marinades that just have three ingredients (not counting the water). Serve this baked tofu dish with Southeast Asian Greens and Noodles (page 101).

2 tablespoons water

2 tablespoons soy sauce

2 tablespoons coconut milk

Freshly squeezed juice of $\frac{1}{2}$ lime

1 pound firm tofu

Preheat the oven to 375°F. Oil a baking sheet.

Put the water, soy sauce, coconut milk, and lime juice in a bowl and stir until thoroughly combined. Cut the tofu into slabs $\frac{1}{4}$ inch thick. Dip each slab in the sauce, then arrange the tofu on the prepared baking sheet. Bake for 30 minutes, until it starts to brown.

144 THE ACCIDENTAL VEGAN

COCONUT-TAMARIND BAKED TOFU

Here tamarind, which hails from a tropical tree, contributes a sweet-and-sour taste. The coconut milk nicely rounds out its flavor.

2 tablespoons water

2 tablespoons soy sauce

2 tablespoons coconut milk

$\frac{1}{2}$ teaspoon tamarind concentrate

1 pound firm tofu

Preheat the oven to 375°F. Oil a baking sheet.

Put the water, soy sauce, coconut milk, and tamarind paste in a bowl and stir until thoroughly combined. Cut the tofu into slabs $\frac{1}{4}$ inch thick. Dip each slab in the sauce, then spread the tofu on the prepared baking sheet. Bake for 30 minutes, until it starts to brown.

SMOKY MISO BAKED TOFU

If you'd like, you can substitute Bragg Liquid Aminos for soy sauce in this recipe. It's not quite as salty, and its fermented flavor works nicely with the miso, which is also fermented. You can use any type of miso in this marinade; experiment and see what you like best.

3 tablespoons water

2 tablespoons tahini

1 tablespoon soy sauce

1 teaspoon miso

$1/2$ teaspoon liquid smoke

1 pound firm tofu

Preheat the oven to 375°F. Oil a baking sheet.

Put the water, tahini, soy sauce, miso, and liquid smoke in a bowl and stir until thoroughly combined. Cut the tofu into slabs $1/4$ inch thick. Dip each slab in the sauce, then arrange the tofu on the prepared baking sheet. Bake for 30 minutes, until it starts to brown.

TOMATO-BASIL BAKED TOFU

MAKES 4 SERVINGS

Here the classic Italian flavors of tomato and basil flavor a very un-Italian protein.

$\frac{1}{2}$ cup tomato juice

1 tablespoon balsamic vinegar

1 tablespoon chopped basil

1 pound firm tofu

Preheat the oven to 375°F. Oil a baking sheet.

Put the tomato juice, vinegar, and basil in a bowl and stir until thoroughly combined. Cut the tofu into slabs $\frac{1}{4}$ inch thick. Dip each slab in the sauce, then arrange the tofu on the prepared baking sheet. Bake for 30 minutes, until it starts to brown.

CAJUN SPICE BAKED TOFU

Serve this spicy tofu with brown rice and Cajun Greens (page 173).

$1/2$ cup tomato juice

1 teaspoon prepared mustard

1 teaspoon Vegan Worcestershire Sauce (page 35)

$1/2$ teaspoon hot sauce (optional)

1 pound firm tofu

Preheat the oven to 375°F. Oil a baking sheet.

Put the tomato juice, mustard, Worcestershire sauce, and hot sauce in a bowl and stir until thoroughly combined. Cut the tofu into slabs $1/4$ inch thick. Dip each slab in the sauce, then arrange the tofu on the prepared baking sheet. Bake for 30 minutes, until it starts to brown.

SPINACH AND TOFU IN PEANUT SAUCE

This is a lovely, layered dish with crunchy tofu and spicy peanut sauce on a bed of fresh spinach. Serve with rice or rice noodles. The recipe calls for whole wheat pastry flour, but you can use any flour you have on hand.

Peanut or canola oil for frying

8 ounces firm tofu

1/4 cup whole wheat pastry flour

1 bunch spinach, cleaned and stemmed

2 cups Peanut Sauce (page 32)

In a small skillet, heat 1 inch of oil over medium-low heat for deep-frying (see Basic Techniques, page 219, for tips on deep-frying). Cut the tofu in bite-sized cubes and gently roll the pieces in the flour. When the oil is hot (about 360°F), carefully lower the tofu into the oil using a slotted spoon, and fry for about 5 minutes, until golden brown.

Meanwhile, steam the spinach for about 1 minute, until just wilted.

Remove the tofu from the oil with a slotted spoon and drain on paper towels or clean brown bags. Arrange the spinach on a serving plate, put the tofu on top, and spoon the peanut sauce over it all. Serve right away.

BASIC SEITAN

MAKES 2 POUNDS

Seitan is, well, a meat substitute. I prefer seitan rather than tofu in many recipes because it's less likely to fall apart, and it accepts flavor just as well as tofu does. Made from wheat gluten, seitan is high in protein and low in fat. If you have the right ingredients, it's relatively easy to make. The most important thing is to use gluten flour, which is also known as high-gluten flour or 80 percent gluten flour. Over years of feeding vegetarians, it's been my experience that people generally either love seitan or hate it. If you hate it, skip it. If you love it, you'll be happy with this recipe, which is easier than any I've read. If it's new to you, give it a try. It's quite versatile. You can store leftovers in the refrigerator in the broth it was cooked in. It will keep for about 10 days.

4 quarts water

1 (2-Inch) piece of ginger

$1/2$ cup soy sauce

1 cup gluten flour

1 to 2 cups warm water

Put the 4 quarts water, ginger, and soy sauce in a large stock pot and bring to a boil over high heat. In a large bowl, combine the gluten flour and 1 cup of the warm water in a bowl and mix with your hands until it becomes a sticky blob. Add more of the warm water as needed, mixing as you add it, until some water starts to collect in the bottom of the bowl. Run more warm water over the gluten and knead it underwater for a few minutes, changing the water when it gets cloudy. If the gluten flour you use is fresh, the dough will hold together. If It Isn't fresh, it will break apart as you knead it. If this happens, strain the gluten in a sieve, then collect the pieces and press them back together.

(continued)

Basic Seitan, continued

When the water in the stockpot boils, break off pieces of gluten about the size of a peanut and drop them into the pot. Cook for about 1 hour, then remove the pieces with a slotted spoon. If you're making the seitan in advance to have on hand, turn off the heat, let the seitan and liquid stand for about an hour to cool down, then transfer to a container and put in the refrigerator to continue cooling.

SEITAN SATAY

MAKES 12 TO 15 SKEWERS

Who says vegans can't participate in the primeval joy of meat on a stick? You'll need 12 to 15 wooden skewers for this dish. Serve with Pad Thai (page 102).

1 pound Basic Seitan (page 149), cut in bite-sized chunks

2 cups Peanut Sauce (page 32)

Preheat the oven to 400°F, or if you're going to grill on an open flame, prepare a medium-hot grill. For grilling, soak the skewers in water while you prepare the seitan and peanut sauce.

Combine the seitan and 1 cup of the peanut sauce in a bowl, toss to combine, then thread 7 to 8 pieces of seitan on each skewer.

Roast the skewers on a baking pan for 15 to 20 minutes, until they start to brown. Alternatively, grill them for about 2 minutes, then turn them and grill them for two more minutes. Serve right away, with the rest of the peanut sauce alongside, for dipping.

KUNG PAO SEITAN

MAKES 6 SERVINGS

Serve this Chinese dish of seitan, veggies, and cashews with Fried Rice (page 190).

1 tablespoon olive oil

1 onion, minced

2 cloves garlic, minced

1 tablespoon grated ginger

3 tablespoons soy sauce

2 carrots, chopped

1 zucchini, chopped

1 cup chopped bok choy

6 mushrooms, quartered

8 ounces chopped Basic Seitan (page 149)

1 (5-ounce) can sliced water chestnuts, drained

1 (5-ounce) can bamboo shoots, drained

1 cup bean sprouts

1 teaspoon toasted sesame oil

¼ cup cashews

Chili oil

Heat the olive oil in a saucepan or skillet over medium-low heat, add the onion, garlic, and ginger, and sauté for about 5 minutes, until the onion is soft. Stir in the soy sauce and carrots, cook a few more minutes, then stir in the zucchini, bok choy, and mushrooms and cook, stirring often, for another 8 to 10 minutes, until the veggies are tender.

Stir in the seitan, water chestnuts, bamboo shoots, bean sprouts, sesame oil, and cashews, then season to taste with chili oil. Cook, stirring occasionally, for another 5 minutes. Serve hot.

THAI CURRY WITH SEITAN

This Thai stir-fry features a wide range of veggies and the flowery taste of lemongrass. You can substitute firm tofu for seitan in this recipe if you like. Even if you don't use the lemongrass or lime leaves, the dish will still be tasty. Serve with jasmine rice.

3 tablespoons soy sauce

2 tablespoons freshly squeezed lime juice

8 ounces Basic Seitan (page 149), cut in bite-sized chunks

1 tablespoon olive oil

1 onion, diced

4 cloves garlic, minced

3 tablespoons grated ginger

3 stalks lemongrass, cut in 2- to 3-inch pieces

6 to 8 kaffir lime leaves

2 carrots, sliced

2 cups cauliflower, chopped

2 cups broccoli, chopped

2 zucchini, sliced

1 baby bok choy, chopped

8 mushrooms, quartered

1 cup green beans, chopped

2 tablespoons coconut milk

Put the soy sauce and lime juice in a shallow bowl, stir to combine, then stir in the seitan and marinate for at least 20 minutes.

Heat the oil in a wok or large skillet over medium-low heat, then add the onion, garlic, ginger, lemongrass, and lime leaves, and sauté for 3 to 5 minutes, until the onion is soft. Pour in half of the seitan marinade, then add the carrots, cauliflower, and broccoli and sauté for 5 minutes. Add the zucchini, bok choy, mushrooms, and green beans and sauté for 5 to 10 minutes, until the vegetables are tender. Stir in the coconut milk and seitan, along with the remaining marinade, and cook a few minutes longer, until heated through. Pick out the lemongrass and lime leaves and serve hot.

KOREAN BARBECUED SEITAN

Even hard-core carnivores will be satisfied with these chewy chunks of barbecued seitan with roasted marinated onions. Serve this dish with Fried Rice (page 190) and Kim Chee (page 54).

$1/2$ cup soy sauce

1 teaspoon grated ginger

1 tablespoon molasses

$1/2$ teaspoon toasted sesame oil

2 onions, sliced in rings

2 pounds Basic Seitan (page 149), cut in bite-sized chunks

2 tablespoons sesame seeds, hulled or unhulled

Preheat the oven to 400°F.

Combine the soy sauce, ginger, molasses, and sesame oil in a bowl large enough to accommodate the onions and seitan, and whisk to combine. Add the onions and seitan and toss until everything is evenly coated.

Spread the onions and seitan on a baking pan and sprinkle with the sesame seeds. Roast for 30 to 40 minutes, until the onions are tender and start to brown. You can use the remaining marinade as a dipping sauce.

SEITAN CACCIATORE

Here seitan stars in a tomato-based stew that's wonderful ladled over rice or pasta.

2 green bell peppers, cut in strips

2 red bell peppers, cut in strips

4 cups Tomato Sauce (page 24)

2 pounds Basic Seitan (page 149), cut in bite-sized chunks

1 cup frozen peas

Steam the bell peppers for 3 to 4 minutes, until tender. In a separate saucepan, gently heat the tomato sauce, seitan, and peas, stirring occasionally, for 5 to 10 minutes, until the mixture is heated through. Add the peppers, and serve.

SEITAN PEPPER STEAK

MAKES 6 SERVINGS

When I was growing up, pepper steak was my father's favorite meal to prepare. Here's a vegan version I came up with that has a similar look and feel.

1 tablespoon olive oil

2 onions, cut in rings

2 cloves garlic, minced

1 tablespoon grated ginger

2 green bell peppers, cut in strips

2 red bell peppers, cut in strips

2 pounds Basic Seitan (page 149)

3 tablespoons soy sauce

1 teaspoon toasted sesame oil

Heat the olive oil in a wok or large skillet over medium-low
heat, add the onions, garlic, and ginger, and sauté for 5 minutes, until the onions are soft. Stir in the bell peppers, seitan,
and soy sauce, and cook, stirring occasionally, for another
5 to 10 minutes, until the peppers are tender and the seitan is
heated through. Stir in the sesame oil and serve hot.

SEITAN GYROS

MAKES 4 SANDWICHES

We serve this sandwich in my restaurant, where it's a customer favorite. If you can't find pocketless Greek pita, just use regular pita and put the fillings inside, as you would for falafel.

2 tablespoons olive oil, or more as needed

1 teaspoon freshly squeezed lemon juice

$\frac{1}{2}$ teaspoon dried dill

$\frac{1}{2}$ teaspoon sea salt

1 pound Basic Seitan (page 149), chopped

4 loaves Greek pita bread

4 leaves romaine lettuce

2 Roma tomatoes, finely chopped

$\frac{1}{2}$ cup Tahini Dressing (page 48)

Put the oil, lemon juice, dill, and salt in a shallow bowl, stir to combine, then toss the seitan in this marinade. Put a small skillet over medium heat, pour in the seitan and its marinade, and cook and stir for a few minutes, until the seitan starts to brown.

Remove the seitan from the pan and heat each pita in the pan for a few seconds on each side. There should be enough oil left in the pan to keep them from sticking, but if they do stick, add a little more oil.

To assemble the sandwiches, arrange $\frac{1}{2}$ cup of seitan in a row along the length of each pita. Top each with a leaf of lettuce, one-fourth of the chopped tomato, and 2 tablespoons of Tahini Dressing, then roll the pita around it all to make a cone-shaped sandwich.

SEITAN WITH MUSHROOM SAUCE

MAKES 4 SERVINGS

This dish, with its chunks of seitan in a thick, mushroom gravy, is great over Barley with Almonds (page 181) or Acorn Squash Stuffed with Wild Rice (page 166).

1 tablespoon olive oil

1 onion, chopped

3 cloves garlic, minced

8 ounces mushrooms, sliced

1 teaspoon dried thyme

1 teaspoon sea salt

2 tablespoons rice flour, white or brown

1 cup water

2 tablespoons Vegan Worcestershire Sauce (page 35)

8 ounces Basic Seitan (page 149), cut in bite-sized chunks

Heat the oil in a saucepan over medium-low heat, add the onion and garlic, and sauté for about 5 minutes, until the onion is soft. Add the mushrooms, thyme, and salt and sauté for about 10 minutes, until the mushrooms start to release their liquid.

Sprinkle in the flour a bit at a time, stirring all the while, then stir in the water and Worcestershire sauce. Cook, stirring frequently, for about 10 minutes, until the gravy starts to thicken, then stir in the seitan and cook for another 5 minutes, until heated through. Serve hot.

MUSHROOM-POLENTA CASSEROLE

This delicious polenta torte has a layer of herbs and mixed mushrooms in the middle. It's a complete meal with a "meaty" surprise inside.

2 tablespoons olive oil

1 pound mushrooms, quartered

8 ounces shiitake, portobello, oyster, or chanterelle mushrooms, or a combination, sliced

3 shallots, chopped

2 cloves garlic, minced

$1\frac{1}{2}$ teaspoons sea salt

1 bunch Swiss chard, stemmed and chopped

$\frac{1}{2}$ cup white wine

$4\frac{1}{2}$ cups water

$1\frac{1}{2}$ cups polenta

$\frac{1}{2}$ teaspoon dried thyme

$\frac{1}{2}$ teaspoon dried tarragon

$\frac{1}{2}$ teaspoon dried marjoram

Preheat the oven to 350°F.

Heat 1 tablespoon of the olive oil in a saucepan over medium-low heat, add the mushrooms, shallots, garlic, and $\frac{1}{2}$ teaspoon of the salt, and sauté for about 5 minutes, until the shallots are soft. Stir in the chard and wine, turn the heat down to low, and cook, stirring occasionally, for about 5 minutes, until the chard is tender.

(continued)

Mushroom–Polenta Casserole, continued

Combine 2¼ cups of the water with half of the remaining tea-spoon of salt and half of the remaining tablespoon of olive oil in a saucepan over high heat and bring to a boil. Turn down the heat to medium-low and stir in ¾ cup of the polenta, stirring all the while to prevent lumps. Simmer, stirring almost constantly, for 2 to 3 minutes, until the polenta thickens to the consistency of split pea soup. Stir in half of the herbs, pour the mixture into a large casserole pan, and smooth it into an even layer if need be. Let the polenta in the pan set for 10 minutes, until it is just firm to the touch.

Gently spoon the mushroom mixture over the polenta in an even layer.

Cook the remaining polenta according to the instructions above, then pour it on top of the mushroom mixture. Bake, uncovered, for 15 to 20 minutes, until heated through.

COLLARD GREENS AND BLACK-EYED PEAS

Here is my version of a classic Southern comfort food. You can use the stems from the greens or not, depending on your preference (see Pantry, page 210).

4 cups water

2 cups dry black-eyed peas

3 cloves garlic, minced

3 tablespoons Vegan Worcestershire Sauce (page 35)

1/2 teaspoon sea salt

1 bunch collard greens, chopped

Hot sauce

Bring the water to a boil in a saucepan over high heat. Stir in the black-eyed peas, garlic, Worcestershire sauce, and salt, then lower the heat, cover, and simmer for about 30 minutes, until the black-eyed peas are just soft.

Stir in the collard greens and cook for another 20 to 30 minutes, until the greens are very soft and the black-eyed peas start to break down. Season to taste with hot sauce, and more salt if you like. Serve hot.

SWEET POTATO POT PIE

MAKES 8 SERVINGS

I adore this recipe. Polenta on the bottom, curried lentils in the middle, and yams on top. It's great for Thanksgiving—or any day, for that matter. If you're preparing this recipe in advance to serve later, try to stagger the steps enough to let the bottom two layers cool fully before you top them with the yams. Cooling each layer separately will keep the dish from getting soggy from condensation.

YAMS

6 yams

$1/2$ teaspoon sea salt

LENTILS

6 cups water

2 cups lentils

1 onion, chopped

3 cloves garlic, minced

1 tablespoon grated ginger

1 cup canned crushed tomatoes or tomato puree

1 teaspoon ground cinnamon

1 teaspoon ground cumin

1 teaspoon ground coriander

1 teaspoon sea salt

POLENTA

3 cups water

1 tablespoon olive oil

1 teaspoon sea salt

1 cup polenta

To make the yams, preheat the oven to 400°F, then bake the yams for 1 to 1½ hours, until they're very soft. When the yams are cool enough to handle, scoop the flesh into a bowl, sprinkle the salt over them, and mash until smooth. Set aside.

To make the lentils, bring the water to a boil in a saucepan over high heat, then stir in the lentils, onion, garlic, ginger, tomatoes, cinnamon, cumin, coriander, and salt. Lower the heat, cover, and simmer for about 45 minutes, until the lentils are soft and start to break down. Turn off the heat and set the lentils aside.

To make the polenta, combine the water, oil, and salt in a small saucepan over high heat and bring to a boil. Turn down the heat to medium-low and slowly pour in the polenta, stirring all the while to prevent lumps. Simmer, stirring almost constantly, for 2 to 3 minutes, until it thickens to the consistency of split pea soup. Pour the polenta into a large casserole pan and smooth it into an even layer if need be. Let it set for at least 10 minutes, until almost firm to the touch.

Preheat the oven to 350°F. Pour the lentils over the polenta and, if the lentils are hot, let cool for 10 to 15 minutes. Spoon the mashed yams over the lentils in evenly spaced dollops, then gently spread them with the back of a spoon. Bake for 15 minutes, until heated through. If the layers are at room temperature before baking, it may take 20 minutes; if you've prepared the dish in advance and they're chilled, it could take as along as 30 to 40 minutes.

CAJUN RED BEANS AND RICE

MAKES 4 SERVINGS

This is a vegetarian version of the Cajun staple. Vegan sausage and liquid smoke are reminiscent of the Southern flavors traditionally found in this dish.

1 tablespoon olive oil

1 onion, chopped

2 cloves garlic, minced

1 green bell pepper, chopped

1½ cups cooked small red beans, or 1 (15-ounce) can, drained

1½ cups cooked brown rice

4 ounces vegan sausage, cut in ½-inch slices

2 tablespoons Vegan Worcestershire Sauce (page 35)

1 teaspoon sea salt

½ teaspoon liquid smoke

Hot sauce

Heat the oil in a skillet or saucepan over medium-low heat, add the onion, garlic, and bell pepper, and sauté for 5 minutes, until the onion is soft. Stir in the beans, rice, vegan sausage, Worcestershire sauce, salt, and liquid smoke and cook for another 5 to 10 minutes, until heated through. Season to taste with hot sauce before serving.

RED BEANS AND GREENS IN COCONUT MILK

MAKES 4 SERVINGS

This dish is one of my personal favorites. It's so simple, and so nutritious. You need to soak the beans for at least a few hours before cooking, so plan ahead. You can use the stems from the greens or not, depending on your preference (see Pantry, page 210).

1 cup small red beans

2 1/2 cups water

1 onion, chopped

1 tomato, chopped

1 teaspoon ground turmeric

1 teaspoon sea salt

3 cups chopped kale, collard greens, mustard greens, or a combination

2 tablespoons coconut milk

Cayenne

Cover the beans in water about 1 inch deep over the beans and let soak for a few hours or overnight.

Drain and rinse the beans, put them in a saucepan, and add the water. Bring to a boil over high heat, then turn the heat down to medium-low and cook for 30 minutes. Stir in the onion, tomato, turmeric, and salt and simmer for another 30 minutes. Stir in the greens and cook for another 15 to 20 minutes, until the beans are very soft. Stir in the coconut milk, season to taste with cayenne, and serve hot.

ACORN SQUASH STUFFED WITH WILD RICE

MAKES 6 SERVINGS

The flavors of squash and wild rice are reminiscent of autumn harvest — one reason why this is a traditional Thanksgiving dish.

6 cups water

1 cup wild rice

1 1/2 cups brown rice

3 acorn squash

1 tablespoon olive oil

1 onion, chopped

1 teaspoon sea salt

1/2 teaspoon freshly ground black pepper

1 bunch parsley, stemmed and chopped

1/2 cup bread crumbs

Preheat the oven to 350°F.

Bring the water to a boil in a saucepan over high heat, then stir in the wild rice, turn the heat down to medium-low, cover, and cook for 30 minutes. Stir in the brown rice, cover, and simmer for about 45 minutes longer, until all of the liquid is absorbed.

Meanwhile, cut the squash in half and scoop out the seeds. Place the squash in a baking pan, pour in 1/2 inch of water, and bake it for 45 minutes to 1 hour, until the squash is soft. Leave the oven on.

While the squash is cooking, heat the oil in a small saucepan over medium-low heat, add the onion, salt, and pepper, and sauté for about 5 minutes, until the onion is soft and translucent.

Stir the onion mixture and parsley into the cooked rice. Scoop out about half of the pulp from each squash, leaving an even layer of pulp in each half. Mash the scooped-out squash, then stir it into the rice. Stuff each of the squash halves with the rice, top with bread crumbs, and bake for 15 minutes, until heated through.

AFGHANI STEW

The first time I tasted Afghan food I knew I absolutely had to learn to make it. The seasonings are subtle yet complex, telling the story of a land that sits at the crossroads of Asia, Eastern Europe, and the Middle East. Serve this dish with Basmati Pilaf (page 188).

2 tablespoons olive oil

1 eggplant, chopped

1 onion, chopped

2 cloves garlic, minced

1 teaspoon dried dill

1 teaspoon ground cumin

1 teaspoon dried mint

1/2 teaspoon ground cardamom

1 teaspoon sea salt

2 carrots, chopped

1 zucchini, chopped

1 cup canned crushed tomatoes

1 bunch spinach, cleaned and stemmed

1 tablespoon chopped cilantro

1 tablespoon freshly squeezed lemon juice, or more to taste

Heat the oil in a large skillet over medium-low heat, then stir in the eggplant, onion, garlic, dill, cumin, mint, cardamom, and salt. Sauté for about 10 minutes, until the eggplant is soft, adding a few tablespoons of water if the eggplant sticks to the pan. Stir in the carrots, sauté for a few minutes, then stir in the zucchini. Cook for 5 minutes longer, until all the veggies are tender, then stir in the tomatoes and spinach and cook for another 5 minutes, until the zucchini is tender. Stir in the cilantro and lemon juice and serve hot.

BEAN AND BASIL BURGERS

Even children enjoy these burgers. If you want them to look more homogeneous, you can chop all of the ingredients together in a food processor or blender. Serve them on buns with whatever condiments and fixings you prefer.

2 cups cooked black beans, or 1 (15-ounce) can, drained

2 cups cooked brown rice

3 tablespoons chopped black olives

2 tablespoons chopped basil

2 tablespoons tomato paste

1 tablespoon crushed red pepper (optional)

$\frac{1}{2}$ teaspoon sea salt

Preheat the oven to 350°F. Grease a baking sheet.

Combine all of the ingredients in a bowl and mix with your hands. Form the mixture into burgers, wetting your hands as needed to prevent sticking. For more perfectly shaped burgers, you can use an ice cream scoop to make round balls and then flatten them.

Put the patties on the prepared baking sheet and bake for 10 to 15 minutes, until they just start to get crusty on top.

SIDE DISHES

Vegetable Dishes

Grain Dishes

EGGPLANT FILLETS

MAKES 6 SERVINGS

Crispy on the outside, tender on the inside, these fillets go well with Spana-kopita (page 131) or Greek Lasagna (page 106).

1 eggplant, sliced $\frac{1}{4}$ inch thick

4 tablespoons olive oil

1 tablespoon freshly squeezed lemon juice

$\frac{1}{2}$ teaspoon dried dill

$\frac{1}{2}$ teaspoon sea salt

Preheat the oven to 375°F.

With a pastry brush, cover the bottom of a baking sheet with some of the olive oil, then arrange the eggplant slices on the pan in a single layer. Combine the remaining olive oil with the lemon juice, dill, and salt in a small bowl and whisk until emulsified, then brush the mixture on top of the eggplant slices.

Bake for 10 to 15 minutes, until the eggplant is tender.

SZECHUAN EGGPLANT

MAKES 4 SERVINGS

Nothing holds flavor as fully as eggplant. Here it soaks up spicy Chinese seasonings. Serve with Lo Mein (page 98).

2 tablespoons olive oil

1 eggplant, cut in bite-sized pieces

1 onion, chopped

2 cloves garlic, minced

1 tablespoon grated ginger

2 tablespoons soy sauce

1 tablespoon rice vinegar

1 teaspoon toasted sesame oil

$1/2$ teaspoon raw sugar

Chili oil

Heat the olive oil in a wok or skillet over medium-low heat, add the eggplant, onion, garlic, and ginger, and sauté for 10 to 15 minutes, until the eggplant is soft. Stir in the soy sauce, vinegar, sesame oil, and sugar and cook, stirring occasionally, for another 5 minutes, until heated through. Season to taste with chili oil and serve hot.

ROASTED VEGGIES

MAKES 6 SERVINGS

Roasting brings out the flavor of vegetables to the fullest. I like to parboil the veggies first because it gives the harder vegetables a head start, allowing you to roast everything together for the same length of time. My favorite vegetables to roast are onions, fennel, and parsnips. Serve Roasted Veggies as a side dish with any kind of lasagna.

Choose your favorites from the following veggies and prepare a total of about 3 pounds combined weight:

Red or Yukon gold potatoes (unpeeled), chopped

Carrots, sliced

Parsnips, sliced

Fennel, cored and chopped

Red or yellow onion, cut in rings

Red or green bell peppers, cut in strips

1/4 cup chopped basil

2 tablespoons olive oil

1 teaspoon sea salt

1/2 teaspoon freshly ground black pepper

Preheat the oven to 400°F.

Fill a saucepan about two-thirds full with water and bring to boil over high heat. Add the potatoes and boil for 3 minutes, then add the carrots and parsnips and boil for another 2 minutes. Drain the vegetables.

Combine the basil, oil, salt, and pepper in a large bowl and stir to blend. Add all of the vegetables and toss until evenly coated. Spread the veggies on a baking sheet, then roast them on the top rack of the oven for 20 to 30 minutes, until they're tender and start to brown. Serve hot.

CAJUN GREENS

MAKES 6 SERVINGS

I like to cook these particular greens until they're very, very soft, like traditional Southern fare. You can use the stems from the greens or not, depending on your preference (see Pantry, page 210). Serve with Cajun Red Beans and Rice (page 164).

1½ tablespoons olive oil

1 onion, chopped

2 cloves garlic, minced

1 tomato, chopped

1 bunch collard greens, chopped

1 bunch kale or mustard greens, chopped

1 bunch Swiss chard, chopped

1 bunch spinach, cleaned and stemmed

1 teaspoon sea salt

2 tablespoons Vegan Worcestershire Sauce (page 35)

Hot sauce

Heat the oil in a soup pot or large skillet over medium-low heat, add the onion, garlic, and tomato, and sauté for about 5 minutes, until the onion is soft. Add the greens, one variety at a time. After adding each one, cook and stir until it cooks down and you have room in the pan to add the next. Once all of the greens have been added, stir in the salt and Worcestershire sauce, cover, and cook, stirring occasionally, for 15 to 20 minutes, until the greens are very soft. Season to taste with hot sauce before serving.

COLLARD GREENS WITH GINGER AND TOMATO

MAKES 4 SERVINGS

Here collard greens are seasoned with ingredients common in East African cuisine. You can use the stems from the greens or not, depending on your preference (see Pantry, page 210). This dish is the perfect complement to Sweet Potato Pot Pie (page 162).

1 tablespoon olive oil

1/2 onion, chopped

1 tablespoon grated ginger

1 teaspoon ground cumin

1/2 teaspoon ground coriander

Pinch of ground cinnamon

1 tomato, chopped

1 bunch collard greens, chopped

Sea salt

Heat the oil in a large saucepan over medium-low heat, add the onion, ginger, cumin, coriander, and cinnamon, and sauté for about 5 minutes, until the onion is soft. Stir in the tomato and cook, stirring occasionally another 5 minutes, until it starts to break down, then stir in the collard greens and cook, stirring occasionally, for 10 to 15 minutes, until they're soft. Season with salt to taste before serving.

ITALIAN GREENS

Greens sautéed with basil and garlic are a classic Italian dish that goes well with any type of lasagna. You can use the stems from the greens or not, depending on your preference (see Pantry, page 210).

1 tablespoon olive oil

3 cloves garlic, minced

1 teaspoon sea salt

$1/2$ teaspoon freshly ground black pepper

1 bunch collard greens, chopped

1 bunch kale, chopped

1 bunch Swiss chard, chopped

1 bunch mustard greens, chopped

1 bunch spinach, cleaned and stemmed

1 cup loosely packed basil leaves

Heat the oil in a soup pot or large skillet over medium-low heat, add the garlic, and sauté for about 1 minute. Sprinkle in the salt and pepper, then add the greens, one variety at a time. After adding each one, cook and stir until it cooks down and you have room in the pan to add the next. Once all of the greens have been added, lower the heat to low, cover, and cook for 5 minutes, until the greens are soft. Stir in the basil and cook a minute or two longer. Serve hot.

GREEK POTATOES

These lemony potatoes, prepared with garlic and Greek seasonings, make a nice accompaniment for Spanakopita (page 131) or Greek Lasagna (page 106).

6 to 8 red potatoes (unpeeled), chopped

1 tablespoon olive oil

2 cloves garlic, minced

2 tablespoons chopped mint

2 tablespoons chopped dill

1 tablespoon freshly squeezed lemon juice, or more to taste

1 teaspoon sea salt

$1/2$ teaspoon freshly ground black pepper

Put the potatoes in a saucepan, add water to cover by an inch or two, and bring to a boil over high heat. Lower the heat to medium, cover, and cook for 10 minutes, until tender.

Meanwhile, heat the oil in a small skillet over medium-low heat, add the garlic, and sauté for a minute or two. Remove from the heat and stir in the mint, dill, lemon juice, salt, and pepper.

Drain the potatoes, pour in the garlic and seasonings, and stir gently. Serve hot.

POTATOES WITH CHILES

Serve these potatoes with salsa, or as a side dish for any south-of-the-border-style stew.

6 to 8 Yukon gold, red, or yellow Finn potatoes (unpeeled), chopped

3 tablespoons diced mild green chiles, canned or fresh

2 tablespoons chopped cilantro

1 teaspoon sea salt

Put the potatoes in a saucepan, add water to cover by an inch or two, and bring to a boil over high heat. Lower the heat to medium, cover, and cook for about 10 minutes, until soft.

Drain the potatoes, put them in a serving dish, and stir in the chiles, cilantro, and salt. Serve hot.

ROASTED POTATOES

MAKES 6 SERVINGS

Try these potatoes with Bean and Basil Burgers (page 168).

2 pounds red, yellow Finn, or Yukon gold potatoes (unpeeled), chopped

2 tablespoons chopped dill

2 tablespoons olive oil

$1/2$ teaspoon sea salt

$1/2$ teaspoon freshly ground black pepper

Preheat the oven to 400°F. Oil a baking sheet.

Put the potatoes in a saucepan, add water to cover by an inch or two, and bring to a boil over high heat. Lower the heat to medium, cover, and cook for 5 minutes.

Drain the potatoes, stir in the dill, oil, salt, and pepper, and spread in an even layer on the prepared baking sheet. Roast for about 20 minutes, until they're tender and start to brown. Serve hot.

WINTER SQUASH WITH HERBS

This sweet and creamy dish hits the same spot as mashed potatoes. Use it as a side dish with pasta or a casserole.

2 acorn squash

2 tablespoons chopped basil

2 tablespoons chopped parsley

1 tablespoon freshly squeezed lemon juice, or more to taste

1 teaspoon sea salt

Freshly ground black pepper

Preheat the oven to 400°F.

Cut the squash in half and scoop out the seeds. Place the squash in a baking pan cut side down, pour in $1/2$ inch of water, and bake for about 1 hour, until the squash is very soft.

When the squash is cool enough to handle, scoop the flesh into a bowl and stir in the basil, parsley, lemon juice, and salt. Season to taste with pepper and serve hot.

GINGERED YAMS

MAKES 4 SERVINGS

I have a Brazilian friend who taught me to eat yams with curry powder. The ginger and lime juice were natural additions. Serve with Caribbean Black-Eyed Pea Salad (page 67).

3 yams

1 teaspoon grated ginger

1 tablespoon freshly squeezed lime juice

$1/2$ teaspoon curry powder

Sea salt

Preheat the oven to 400°F.

Bake the yams for 1 to $1^1/_2$ hours, until they're very soft.

When the yams are cool enough to handle, scoop the flesh into a bowl, add the ginger, lime juice, and curry powder, and mash everything together. Season to taste with salt and serve hot.

BARLEY WITH ALMONDS

MAKES 4 SERVINGS

This barley pilaf goes well with Afghani Stew (page 167).

2 cups Veggie Stock (page 74) or water

1 cup pearled barley

2 tablespoons chopped parsley

1 teaspoon sea salt

Pinch of freshly ground black pepper

1/4 cup slivered almonds, roasted (see Pantry, page 211)

Bring the stock to a boil in a small saucepan over high heat, then stir in the barley, parsley, salt, and pepper. Lower the heat, cover, and simmer for about 20 to 30 minutes, until all of the liquid is absorbed. Stir in the almonds and serve hot.

BULGUR PILAF

MAKES 4 SERVINGS

This nutty, cracked wheat pilaf goes well with Smoky Miso Baked Tofu (page 145).

2 cups bulgur wheat

3 cups boiling water

1 tablespoon olive oil

1/2 onion, chopped

1 clove garlic, minced

1 tablespoon chopped parsley

1/4 cup raw sunflower seeds

3/4 teaspoon sea salt

Put the bulgur in a serving bowl, pour in the boiling water, cover tightly, and let sit for about 15 minutes, until all of the liquid is absorbed.

Meanwhile, heat the oil in a small skillet over medium-low heat, add the onion, garlic, and parsley, and sauté for about 5 minutes, until the onion is soft.

Stir in the sunflower seeds and salt, combine this mixture with the bulgur, and serve warm.

POLENTA WITH FRESH HERBS

There's a common misconception that polenta is difficult to prepare. It really isn't. It's also quite inexpensive and versatile, and you can add almost anything to it. Serve it with a stew on top, or cut slices and pan-fry or broil them, then serve alongside Italian Greens (page 175) or Eggplant Parmesan (page 137).

3 cups water

1 tablespoon olive oil

1 teaspoon sea salt

1 cup polenta

2 tablespoons chopped basil

2 tablespoons chopped parsley

To make the polenta, combine the water, oil, and salt in a small saucepan over high heat and bring to a boil. Turn down the heat to medium-low and slowly pour in the polenta, stirring all the while to prevent lumps. Simmer, stirring almost constantly, for 2 to 3 minutes, until it thickens to the consistency of split pea soup.

Stir in the basil and parsley and serve right away, or transfer the mixture to a casserole or small loaf pan to set.

POLENTA WITH CHILES

MAKES 4 SERVINGS

Corn is indigenous to Mexico, but polenta is an Italian innovation. This recipe brings together elements of these two fine cuisines.

2 ancho chiles

3 cups water

1 tablespoon olive oil

1 teaspoon sea salt

1 cup polenta

2 tablespoons diced mild green chiles, fresh or canned

1 tablespoon chopped cilantro

Soak the ancho chiles in boiling water for a few minutes, until softened.

To make the polenta, combine the water, oil, and salt in a small saucepan over high heat and bring to a boil. Turn down the heat to medium-low and slowly pour in the polenta, stirring all the while to prevent lumps. Simmer, stirring almost constantly, for 2 to 3 minutes, until it thickens to the consistency of split pea soup.

Drain the ancho chiles, discard the stems, and finely chop the chiles. Stir them into the polenta, along with the green chiles, and cilantro. Serve right away, or transfer the mixture to a casserole or small loaf pan to set.

POLENTA WITH OLIVES AND SUN-DRIED TOMATOES

Serve this hearty polenta dish with Tomato-Basil Baked Tofu (page 146).

8 to 10 sun-dried tomatoes

3 cups water

1 tablespoon olive oil

1 teaspoon sea salt

1 cup polenta

10 to 12 pitted kalamata olives, sliced

2 tablespoons chopped basil

Soak the sun-dried tomatoes in water for a few minutes, until softened.

To make the polenta, combine the water, oil, and salt in a small saucepan over high heat and bring to a boil. Turn down the heat to medium-low and slowly pour in the polenta, stirring all the while to prevent lumps. Simmer, stirring almost constantly, for 2 to 3 minutes, until it thickens to the consistency of split pea soup.

Drain the tomatoes, finely chop them, then stir them into the polenta, along with the olives and basil. Serve right away, or transfer the mixture to a casserole or small loaf pan to set.

KASHA VARNISHKES

MAKES 4 SERVINGS

This was one of my favorite foods when I was a child. Serve it with Borscht (page 90), and Marinated Cucumber Salad (page 51) for an old-fashioned deli meal, vegan style.

1 tablespoon olive oil

$\frac{1}{2}$ onion, chopped

6 to 8 mushrooms, sliced

1 cup buckwheat groats

2 cups Veggie Stock (page 74) or water

$\frac{1}{2}$ cup butterfly pasta

1 teaspoon chopped parsley

1 teaspoon sea salt

Heat the oil in a small saucepan over medium-low heat, add the onion and mushrooms, and sauté for about 5 minutes, until the onion is soft. Stir in the buckwheat and sauté another 2 minutes. Pour in the stock, bring to a boil, then stir in the pasta, parsley, and salt. Lower the heat, cover, and simmer for about 20 minutes, until all of the liquid is absorbed. Serve hot.

CURRIED MILLET

MAKES 4 SERVINGS

Millet is a fluffy, healthy grain. Grains are actually seeds of nutritious grasses, so I like preparing them with other types of seeds, like the sesame seeds and sunflower seeds in this recipe. Serve Curried Millet with any main dish curry, for a change of pace from the traditional rice.

2 cups Veggie Stock (page 74) or water

1 cup millet

2 tablespoons sesame seeds, hulled or unhulled

2 tablespoons raw sunflower seeds

1 teaspoon grated ginger

1 teaspoon curry powder

1 teaspoon sea salt

Bring the stock to a boil in a small saucepan over high heat. Stir in the millet, sesame seeds, sunflower seeds, ginger, curry powder, and salt, then lower the heat, cover, and simmer for about 20 minutes, until all of the liquid is absorbed. Serve hot.

BASMATI PILAF

The fragrance of basmati rice makes this dish an excellent side for Afghan dishes or East Indian curries.

2 cups water

1 cup brown basmati rice

1/3 cup dried currants

1/2 cup sliced or slivered almonds, roasted
(see Pantry, page 211)

1 tablespoon chopped parsley

1 teaspoon sea salt

Bring the water to a boil in a small saucepan over high heat, then stir in the rice, currants, almonds, parsley, and salt. Lower the heat, cover, and simmer for 30 to 40 minutes, until all of the liquid is absorbed. Serve hot.

WILD RICE WITH MUSHROOMS

MAKES 4 TO 6 SERVINGS

This is a satisfying, earthy side dish. Try it with Sesame Baked Tofu (page 138) or Acorn Squash Ratatouille (page 136).

3 1/2 cups water

1/2 cup wild rice

1 cup brown rice

1 tablespoon olive oil

1/2 onion, chopped

2 cloves garlic, minced

8 ounces mushrooms, quartered

1 tablespoon chopped parsley

1 teaspoon sea salt

Bring the water to a boil in a saucepan over high heat, then stir in the wild rice, turn the heat down to medium-low, cover, and cook for 30 minutes. Stir in the brown rice, cover, and simmer for about 45 minutes longer, until all of the liquid is absorbed.

Meanwhile, heat the oil in a small skillet over medium-low heat, add the onion, garlic, mushrooms, parsley, and salt, and sauté for about 10 minutes, until the onion is translucent and the mushrooms begin to release their juice. Stir the veggies into the rice and serve hot.

FRIED RICE

MAKES 4 TO 6 SERVINGS

This is the first dish I ever learned to cook, though it's evolved over the years. Of course it's a great side dish for Chinese fare, such as Kung Pao Seitan (page 151) or Szechuan Eggplant (page 171), or you can serve it as a main dish if you add seitan or tofu.

1 tablespoon olive oil

1 cup brown rice

1 onion, chopped

1 teaspoon grated ginger

1 cup broccoli florets

1 red bell pepper, diced

2 cups Veggie Stock (page 74) or water

2 tablespoons soy sauce, or more to taste

Heat the oil in a saucepan over medium-low heat, add the rice, onion, and ginger, and sauté for about 5 minutes, until the onion is soft. Add the broccoli and bell pepper and sauté for another 5 to 10 minutes, until the veggies are tender. Stir in the stock and soy sauce, bring to a boil, then lower the heat, cover, and simmer for about 30 to 40 minutes, until all of the liquid is absorbed. Serve hot.

SPANISH RICE

MAKES 4 SERVINGS

Serve this as a side with Spanish Veggie Stew (page 133) or steamed veggies with Romesco Sauce (page 26).

2 cups Veggie Stock (page 74) or water

1 cup brown rice

1 tomato, chopped

1 teaspoon paprika

$1/2$ teaspoon dried oregano

$1/2$ teaspoon sea salt

Cayenne

Bring the stock to a boil in a small saucepan over high heat. Stir in the rice, tomato, paprika, oregano, and salt, then lower the heat, cover, and simmer for 30 to 40 minutes, until all of the liquid is absorbed. Season to taste with cayenne, and more salt if you like. Serve hot.

PULAO

MAKES 4 SERVINGS

This dish of rice and peas, East Indian style, is a great accompaniment to Dev's Basic Curry (page 111) and Palak Tofu (page 117).

2 cups Veggie Stock (page 74) or water

1 cup brown basmati rice

$\frac{1}{2}$ cup frozen peas

1 tablespoon grated ginger

1 teaspoon ground cumin

$\frac{1}{2}$ teaspoon ground coriander

$\frac{1}{2}$ teaspoon ground turmeric

$\frac{1}{2}$ teaspoon ground cardamom

1 teaspoon sea salt

Bring the stock to a boil in a small saucepan over high heat, then stir in the rice, peas, ginger, cumin, coriander, turmeric, cardamom, and salt. Once it returns to a boil, lower the heat, cover, and simmer for about 40 minutes, until all of the liquid is absorbed. Serve hot.

ORZO PILAF

MAKES 4 SERVINGS

This pilaf makes a good base for Mediterranean stews. Orzo is a type of pasta that looks like big grains of rice or barley, and in fact, *orzo* means "barley" in Italian. Since this tiny pasta is more prone than other pastas to stick to the pan while you're cooking it, you should stir it nearly constantly. If you find lumps when you strain it, gently break them apart with your hands or the back of a spoon.

8 ounces orzo

1 tablespoon olive oil

1 onion, chopped

2 cloves garlic, minced

1 tablespoon chopped parsley

1 tablespoon chopped dill

1 tablespoon chopped mint

1 tablespoon freshly squeezed lemon juice, or more to taste

$1/2$ teaspoon sea salt

Freshly ground black pepper

Bring a saucepan of salted water to a boil over medium-high heat, stir in the orzo, and cook, stirring frequently, for about 5 minutes, until al dente. Since it's so small, use a sieve to drain it.

Meanwhile, heat the oil in a small saucepan over medium-low heat, add the onion, garlic, parsley, dill, and mint, and sauté for about 1 minute, until the onion is translucent. Combine the pasta and onion mixture in a serving dish, stir in the lemon juice and salt, and season to taste with pepper before serving.

BUTTERFLIES WITH BASIL

MAKES 4 TO 6 SERVINGS

Use this simple but satisfying pasta dish alongside Seitan Cacciatore (page 155) or Acorn Squash Ratatouille (page 136). Butterfly pasta is also known as bowtie or farfalle (Italian for "butterflies").

1 pound butterfly pasta

1 tablespoon olive oil

2 cloves garlic, minced

$\frac{1}{2}$ cup chopped basil

1 teaspoon balsamic vinegar

1 teaspoon sea salt

Freshly ground black pepper

Bring a pot of salted water to a boil over medium-high heat, stir in the pasta, and cook, stirring occasionally, for 10 to 12 minutes, until al dente.

Meanwhile, heat the oil in a small skillet over low heat, add the garlic, and sauté for 1 to 2 minutes. Drain the pasta and put it in a serving dish. Stir in the garlic, basil, vinegar, and salt, and season to taste with pepper. Serve hot.

MARINATED BLACK-EYED PEAS

MAKES 4 SERVINGS

Black-eyed peas are the most flavorful bean I know of. The vinegar in this recipe complements their sweetness. Serve with Cajun Greens (page 173) and Cajun Spice Baked Tofu (page 147).

2 cups cooked black-eyed peas, or 1 (15-ounce) can, drained

1 zucchini or green bell pepper, minced

1/2 red onion, diced

1 tablespoon chopped parsley

3 tablespoons red wine vinegar

1 tablespoon extra-virgin olive oil

1/2 teaspoon sea salt

Freshly ground black pepper

Put the black-eyed peas, zucchini, onion, and parsley in a bowl and stir until thoroughly combined. In a separate small bowl, combine the vinegar, olive oil, and salt and whisk until emulsified. Pour the dressing over the veggies and season with pepper to taste. Serve chilled; or if you'd like to serve this as a hot side dish, heat it in a small saucepan over medium heat, stirring gently a few times, for about 5 minutes, until heated through.

WHITE BEANS IN MISO-HERB SAUCE

MAKES 4 SERVINGS

The miso and herbs in this recipe give the white beans a deep and satisfying flavor. Serve with Polenta with Fresh Herbs (page 183) or Winter Squash with Herbs (page 179).

2 tablespoons olive oil

1 leek, halved lengthwise, cleaned, and chopped

3 cloves garlic, minced

$\frac{1}{2}$ teaspoon salt

2 tablespoons chopped parsley

2 tablespoons chopped basil

2 cups cooked white beans or 1 (15-ounce) can, drained

1 tablespoon miso (any kind)

Heat the olive oil over medium-low heat in a saucepan or skillet, then add the leeks, garlic, and salt. Cook for 5 minutes, stirring often, until the leeks are soft. Add the parsley and basil and cook for another minute, until the herbs are wilted.

Add the beans and cook for 2 to 3 minutes, stirring often, until they're heated through. Add the miso, mix well, and serve.

DESSERTS

DATE-ALMOND RICE PUDDING

MAKES 4 TO 6 SERVINGS

This traditional Middle Eastern dessert features the lovely, exotic flavor of rose water, which you can find at Middle Eastern markets.

2 cups cooked brown rice

$\frac{1}{2}$ cup chopped pitted dates

1 cup rice milk

$\frac{1}{4}$ cup chopped almonds, with skins

2 tablespoons raw sugar

$\frac{1}{2}$ teaspoon vanilla extract

$\frac{1}{2}$ teaspoon rose water

Combine all of the ingredients in a saucepan over medium-low heat. Cook, stirring occasionally, for about 5 minutes, until heated through. Serve warm.

BAKLAVA

Baklava lends itself well to this vegan adaptation, since the original can be excessively rich and sweet. You'll need an 11 by 17-inch baking pan, and a pastry brush will definitely make your life simpler.

1½ cups water

1 cup raw sugar

1 to 2 cups canola oil

1 (1-pound) package phyllo dough (see Pantry, page 213)

2 cups finely chopped walnuts and almonds

1 teaspoon ground cinnamon

Bring the water to a boil in a small saucepan. Lower the heat and stir in the sugar until dissolved to make a smooth syrup. Simmer for about 15 minutes. Meanwhile, brush a layer of oil on an 11 by 17-inch baking pan. (If you don't have a pastry brush, spread the oil with a spoon or a spatula. You'll end up using more, but it'll work.) Spread a sheet of phyllo on the baking pan, brush it with oil, and repeat with 11 more sheets. Don't agonize if some sheets rip or stick together. The final product will look fine.

Preheat the oven to 375°F. Mix the nuts with the cinnamon and 1 cup of the sugar syrup. Spread the nut mixture as evenly and gently as possible over the phyllo, then layer the remaining phyllo over the nuts, brushing each sheet with oil as before.

Score the baklava into thirds lengthwise and fourths crosswise to make 12 rectangles, cutting through about half the layers. Don't cut all the way to the bottom or the filling will ooze out and it will take forever to clean the pan. Score each rectangle on a diagonal to make 24 triangles. Drizzle the remaining syrup along the cuts you've made.

Bake for 30 to 40 minutes, until the top is golden brown. When the baklava is cool, cut all the way through along the lines you scored.

ALMOND-RICE CRISPIES

MAKES 8 PIECES

These bars are not entirely unlike Rice Krispies treats. You can find the rice syrup and barley malt at natural food stores.

2 cups crispy puffed rice cereal

1 cup coarsely chopped almonds, with skins

1 cup brown rice syrup

1/4 cup barley malt

1 teaspoon vanilla extract

Mix the cereal and almonds together in a bowl.

Combine the rice syrup, barley malt, and vanilla in a small saucepan over medium heat and stir and cook for about 3 minutes, until the consistency has thinned a bit.

Gently stir the syrup mixture into the cereal until thoroughly combined, then press the mixture into an 8-inch square pan and allow to cool. Cut into 8 pieces—or however many you like.

MIXED BERRY CRISP

You can make this recipe in winter with frozen berries, but It's best in the middle of the summer, when fresh, local berries are at their peak. Any type of berries, or any combination, will be wonderful.

BOTTOM LAYER

1 cup apple juice

4 cups mixed berries, such as raspberries, blueberries, and strawberries

2 tablespoons raw sugar (optional)

1 tablespoon rice flour, white or brown

TOP LAYER

3/4 cup nonhydrogenated margarine, softened

3/4 cup raw sugar

1 1/4 cups unbleached white or whole wheat flour

1 teaspoon sea salt

1/2 teaspoon baking soda

1 cup rolled oats

Gently heat the apple juice in a saucepan over medium heat, then stir in the berries and sugar, turn the heat down to medium-low, and cook, stirring occasionally, for 10 to 15 minutes, until the berries start to break down. Sprinkle in the rice flour and cook for a few minutes longer, stirring constantly, until the mixture starts to thicken.

Preheat the oven to 375°F.

(continued)

Mixed Berry Crisp, continued

Cream together the margarine and sugar in a bowl. In a separate bowl or measuring cup, mix the wheat flour, salt, and baking soda, then pour into the sugar mixture. Add the oats and mix with your hands until the ingredients are evenly distributed.

Pour the cooked fruit into an 8-inch square baking pan, then spread the oat mixture over it. Bake for about 30 minutes, until the topping starts to brown.

BAKED APPLES

MAKES 6 SERVINGS

This dessert, made entirely with fruit, is a seasonal favorite. Use any variety of apples except Delicious.

6 apples

1 cup raisins

2 cups apple-cranberry or apple-raspberry juice

Preheat the oven to 375°F.

Core the apples and stuff the centers with raisins. Place the apples in a baking pan, baste them with the juice, then pour in the remaining juice. Bake for about 1 hour, until they're soft and droopy.

APPLE-GINGER CAKE

MAKES 8 PIECES

This is a moist, fruity cake with a bit of a kick from the ginger.

1 cup applesauce

1/2 cup nonhydrogenated margarine, softened

1 cup raw sugar

2 cups unbleached white or whole wheat flour

1/2 teaspoon sea salt

1/2 teaspoon baking soda

1/4 cup grated ginger

Preheat the oven to 375°F. Grease an 8-inch square baking pan.

Mix the applesauce with the margarine, then stir in the sugar. In a separate bowl or measuring cup, mix the flour, salt, and baking soda, then pour into the sugar mixture. Stir in the ginger.

Pour the batter into the prepared pan and bake for 30 to 40 minutes, until the top is golden brown and a knife inserted into the center comes out clean.

RASPBERRY THUMBPRINT COOKIES

MAKES 24 COOKIES

You can use any kind of jam in these cookies, which are moist, chewy, and very pretty.

2 cups nonhydrogenated margarine, softened

2 cups raw sugar

$2\frac{1}{2}$ cups oats

$1\frac{1}{2}$ cups unbleached white or whole wheat flour

2 teaspoons baking soda

1 cup raspberry jam

Preheat the oven to 375°F. Grease 2 cookie sheets.

Cream together the margarine and sugar in a bowl. Finely chop 1 cup of the oats in a food processor. In a separate bowl, mix the chopped oats with the flour and baking soda. Stir the oats mixture into the sugar mixture. Add the remaining $1\frac{1}{2}$ cups of oats and mix until the ingredients are evenly distributed.

Shape the dough into balls the size of ping-pong balls, then arrange them on the prepared cookie sheets and partially flatten them. Using your thumb, make an imprint in the center of each cookie, then spoon a little jam into the indentations.

Bake for 10 to 15 minutes, until the cookies just start to brown.

HAZELNUT AND CHOCOLATE CHIP SHORTBREAD

Because shortbread uses no eggs, it lends itself well to vegan interpretations. And you certainly can't go wrong with chocolate and hazelnuts.

1 cup nonhydrogenated margarine, softened

1 cup raw sugar

2 cups unbleached white or whole wheat flour

$1/2$ teaspoon baking soda

$1/2$ cup chopped hazelnuts

$1/2$ cup dark chocolate chips

Preheat the oven to 350°F. Grease a 9 by 13-inch baking pan.

Cream the margarine with the sugar in a bowl. In a separate bowl or measuring cup, mix the flour and baking soda, then stir it into the sugar mixture. Add the hazelnuts and chocolate chips and mix until the ingredients are evenly distributed.

Spread the batter in the prepared pan and bake for about 30 minutes, until a knife inserted into the center comes out clean

COCOA HALVAH

MAKES 6 SERVINGS

This dense, nutty confection is a Middle Eastern classic. You can find the rice syrup in natural food stores.

1 cup sesame seeds, hulled or unhulled

¼ cup tahini

2 tablespoons brown rice syrup

1 teaspoon vanilla extract

2 tablespoons cocoa powder

Grind the sesame seeds in a food processor until they're mostly powdered, which may take up to 5 minutes.

Heat the tahini, rice syrup, vanilla, and cocoa powder gently in a small saucepan over medium-low heat, stirring until the mixture is smooth. Stir in the sesame seeds, then press the mixture into a small loaf pan or a bowl. Once the halvah is cool, cut it into bite-sized pieces.

CHOCOLATE-OAT BARS

These bars have a dense layer of chocolate on top of a chewy oat and flour crust. I sell them in my shop and folks are always asking for the recipe.

$3/4$ cup nonhydrogenated margarine, softened

$3/4$ cup raw sugar

$1 3/4$ cups unbleached white or whole wheat flour

1 teaspoon sea salt

$1/2$ teaspoon baking soda

1 cup rolled oats

12 ounces dark chocolate chips

Preheat the oven to 375°F.

Cream together the margarine and sugar in a bowl. In a separate bowl or measuring cup, mix the flour, salt, and baking soda, then pour into the sugar mixture. Add the oats and mix with your hands until the ingredients are evenly distributed. The dough will be crumbly, but it should hold together when you squeeze it.

Press two-thirds of this mixture into a smooth layer in the bottom of an 8-inch square pan and bake for about 10 minutes, until it starts to set.

Spread the chocolate chips over the crust, then put the pan back in the oven for about 2 minutes, until the chocolate just starts to melt. Use the back of a spoon to spread the melted chocolate over the crust, then sprinkle the remaining oat mixture evenly over the top. Bake for about 20 minutes longer, until the topping just starts to brown.

PANTRY

Asian Noodles: Some stores sell fresh (refrigerated) Asian noodles that don't have egg in them, but they're hard to find. If you can find these, they'll be great in any recipe in this book that calls for Asian wheat noodles (as opposed to rice noodles). Alternatively, you can use the dried wheat noodles available in Asian markets. I'm not convinced that they're actually different from spaghetti, but the fact that they're marketed as Asian products makes me think they're somehow suited to Asian noodle dishes. Feel free to use spaghetti.

Asparagus: The quintessential spring vegetable, asparagus has a delicate flavor and an exquisite texture—unless you overcook it. You should trim the white end off of each stalk of asparagus. If you bend the stalk, it will break at precisely the point where it becomes tender. Always eat asparagus in season: that way you'll get the highest quality as well as the lowest cost.

Balsamic Vinegar: Most of the products that we buy bearing the name "balsamic vinegar" are actually imitations of an Italian condiment made from grape must that takes at least a dozen years to achieve its characteristic flavor. The widely available imitation products are tasty and affordable and work quite well in most recipes, but I recommend tasting the real thing if you have the opportunity. When choosing among the commercial imitations, it's best to get one that doesn't contain caramel.

Basil: There are two main types of fresh basil available. Thai basil is similar to Italian, or Genovese, basil, but it has pointier, redder leaves, and a mintier flavor. You can substitute Italian basil in Thai recipes, but avoid substituting Thai basil in Italian recipes because the flavor is too strong.

Black Sesame Seeds: A variety of sesame seeds widely used in Chinese and Japanese cuisines, black sesame seeds taste a lot like the tan ones, but they add extra color to dishes. You can find black sesame seeds in Asian groceries and natural food stores.

Cabbage: There are many varieties of cabbage available, from the leafy Asian varieties to the dense green and purple heads that we use in coleslaw. Cabbages absorb flavor well, and can be served either raw or cooked. They are also commonly fermented, as in German sauerkraut, or Korean kim chee. Choose heads of cabbage with darker outer leaves. You don't eat the outermost leaves, but the heads that still have them attached tend to be freshest on the inside.

Carrots: These sweet root vegetables can be enjoyed raw, in salads, or cooked in soups or stews. They're especially tasty roasted. We tend to take them for granted because they're so common, but I certainly wouldn't want to cook without them. They're sweetest during the winter, when plants direct most of their energy underground. You can buy them efficiently trimmed, or with their leaves and stems attached. I hear that the leaves are edible, but I've never tasted them. You can peel carrots, giving them a cleaner taste, but the skins do have plenty of nutrients, so alternately you can just scrub them well and save yourself the extra work of peeling them.

Chili Oil: Usually made from soybean or sesame oil mixed with chili extract, chili oil is commonly used to make Asian foods spicy. It has a nice flavor, and adds a moderate—but not intense—level of heat. Chili oil is usually added to a dish late in the cooking process, often right before it is served.

Chipotles in Adobo: Also called "smoked jalapenos," chipotle chiles are often sold in small cans, with a spicy, brown, garlicky sauce called "adobo." They're intense, so use them sparingly if you're sensitive to spicy foods. Their smoky flavor makes them a useful ingredient in recipes where you're trying to create flavors reminiscent of smoked meats. As with handling any spicy food, wear rubber gloves if you wear contact lenses, and even if you don't, be careful about touching your eyes for a few hours after you handle the chiles.

Cucumber: Crunchy and refreshing; cucumbers work well in any kind of salad. Conventional slicing cucumbers tend to be waxed and should be peeled; the organic ones are often unwaxed, so you can leave the peels on them if you prefer. The longer, English cucumbers have softer skins and don't need to be peeled.

Curry Powder: A spice blend commonly used in east and south Asian dishes, curry powder commonly makes use of cumin, coriander, turmeric, and cardamom, among other spices. Some varieties are mild, while others can be quite spicy. In curries you can either use a prepared curry powder or make your own blend, tailoring it to your individual taste. I generally recommend substituting $2\frac{1}{2}$ teaspoons of curry powder for 1 teaspoon cumin and $\frac{1}{2}$ teaspoon each of turmeric, cardamom, and coriander.

Eggplant: A midsummer gem related to tomatoes and peppers, eggplants are used in quite a few Mediterranean and Asian dishes. Japanese eggplants are smaller than the ones available in most supermarkets, and cook more quickly. Choose eggplants that are firm, but not too firm. They soak up plenty of oil, which can make them quite rich and meaty. Always make sure that you cook eggplants fully: it's better to overcook them than to undercook them.

Fennel: Also known as anise, this tasty bulb is a relative of licorice, and has a sweet, strong flavor. Cut the bulbs in half lengthwise and remove the dense heart before chopping the white part around it. The stems tend to be tough and chewy, but you can finely chop the feathery leaves and add them to Mediterranean-style dishes.

Garlic: Look for garlic bulbs with large cloves: it's much less work to peel a few large cloves than a lot of small ones. You can smash bulbs of garlic with the flat side of a knife, which makes the peels come off easily. Some experts say that this compromises the flavor of the garlic but, if that is the case, it's so subtle that I can't taste the difference.

Greens: You can cut the stems out of the center of hardy, leafy greens, or you can leave them in. Personally, I like to push the envelope and use as much of the vegetable as possible in my cooking. I like to use chard stems, which are colorful as well as tender. Kale stems can be pretty tough, even when they're well cooked. Some people remove the stems from their greens, cut them up, and cook them early in the process, along with the onions and garlic, to make them really tender. Experiment and get to know your personal preferences.

Hot Sauce: There are countless varieties of bottled hot sauce available these days; in fact, there are conventions and festivals dedicated entirely to hot sauce and its aficionados. Tabasco is probably the most widely recognized brand name, which is no accident since they've put quite a bit of money and energy into establishing their dominance in the marketplace, even suing competitors who use their signature Tabasco pepper. In any case, if you like hot food you should check out some of the different varieties and find one that suits your taste. They range from relatively mild to extra hot, and many incorporate additional flavors such as fruit and garlic.

Kaffir Lime Leaves: This variety of lime tree is most commonly used for its fragrant leaves, rather than for its fruit. You can find the leaves in Asian grocery stores and these days even in some mainstream supermarkets. They are sold fresh, dried, or frozen. These leaves—in any form—can be added to Southeast Asian dishes early in the cooking process so that their exquisite flavor infuses the other ingredients. They're generally removed before the dish is served, however, because they can be rather chewy.

Leeks: These hardy members of the onion family have been cultivated since ancient times. They offer the same kind of deep flavor as onions, without being quite as pungent. Trim the hairy tops off your leeks, as well as the tips of the dark green ends. Cut them in half lengthwise and clean well between the outer layers before you slice them because they tend to have a lot of dirt in there.

Lemongrass: Also known as "citronella," lemongrass has a flowery flavor and scent that is used in traditional Southeast Asian recipes. It comes in stalks, which should be trimmed and cut in lengths of two or three inches. In most recipes you don't actually eat the lemongrass because it can be quite tough; cook it into the dish for flavor, and then pick it out at the end.

Margarine: Once hailed as a substitute for cholesterol-laden butter, margarine has come under fire from health experts lately because it contains artificially saturated fat and artificial trans fat, which have been linked to cardiovascular disease. There are varieties available these days that are free from these harmful ingredients. I use them for vegan baking because they make baked dishes fluffy in much the same way as butter.

Miso: Made from fermented soybeans sometimes mixed with rice or barley, miso is a traditional Japanese food that has been linked to a range of health benefits, from lowering blood pressure to strengthening the immune system. It is most often used in soup. Raw (or unpasteurized) miso contains beneficial microorganisms that can be killed if you cook them at too high a temperature, so you should turn off the flame under whatever you're cooking before you add miso. If you do heat miso past the boiling point it'll still taste good, but it's best to keep an eye on the temperature when you're cooking with it.

Nutritional Yeast: Also known as "brewer's yeast" (although the two products are not the same), nutritional yeast grew popular with the spread of the natural foods movement in the 1960s and 1970s. It is high in B vitamins and has a deep, nutty flavor. You can usually find it in the bulk foods section of natural food stores and quality grocery stores.

Nuts: You can buy your nuts already roasted, or you can roast them yourself. Roasting nuts gives them extra, deeper flavor, although raw nuts have plenty of flavor as well. To dry-roast nuts, spread them on a baking sheet and roast them for a minute or two at 400°F, just until you can smell them. Once you have roasted the nuts, you can also remove the skins if you prefer (some people find the skins bitter). Simply rub the roasted nuts gently with a towel and the skins should come off easily. If you buy your nuts already roasted, try to get them from a store that sells plenty of nuts, like a busy natural food store or a gourmet supermarket. Roasted nuts tend to become rancid faster than the raw nuts, and the ones you find at these stores probably won't have sat on the shelf for very long. Dry-roasted nuts are lower in fat than those that have been roasted in oil.

Olive Oil: One of the world's great cooking oils, olive oil has been used in Mediterranean dishes since ancient times; in fact, it was one of the first food items widely traded between far-flung regions. In recent years it has received a good deal of attention as a particularly healthy cooking fat, one that has been linked to cardiovascular health. Olive oils range from very expensive, extra-virgin varieties from the olives' first pressing, to cheaper, "pomace" oils, which are extracted after the finer, more delicate oils have already been squeezed out of the olive. Olive oil has a lower smoke point than some other vegetable oils, such as peanut and canola oils. It shouldn't be used for deep-frying, but you can certainly sauté with it, especially if you don't turn the heat up too high. I tend to use inexpensive olive oil for cooking, and fine, extra-virgin olive oil in salads, where you can really taste it.

Onions: These hardy bulbs are indispensable in a wide range of soups and stews. There are sweet varieties available with a mellower flavor, and also red onions mild enough to be used in salads. I've heard all kinds of tricks for making your eyes burn less when you cut onions, from refrigerating them before you chop them, to using a very sharp knife, to breathing through your mouth. I've never found any of these strategies to be particularly effective, but it has been my experience that the more onions you cut, the less they bother you.

Parsley: You can buy either curly leaf parsley, or flat leaf, Italian parsley. Curly leaf parsley tends to be crunchier, and is best in salads and Middle Eastern recipes. Flat leaf parsley, which looks a lot like cilantro, has more flavor than the curly variety, but not as much texture. It's best for recipes where the parsley is cooked. Ultimately, though, you can easily substitute one kind for another, except in tabouli, where you really should use the curly kind.

Parsnips: A root vegetable available during the fall and winter, parsnips have a deep, sweet flavor that is excellent roasted and also in soups. I peel my parsnips when using them in a dish where they'll be identifiable, such as roasted veggies, but I don't bother when they're going into a stock or a soup where they'll be pureed. Choose small and medium-sized parsnips, as the large ones tend to be woody in the center. Don't ever eat parsnips raw.

Peppers: Members of the chile family, bell peppers are very sweet and can be served raw, in salads, or cooked in stews or stir-fries. They're especially tender when roasted. You can buy roasted red and yellow bell peppers in cans or jars, or you can roast them yourself in the oven, under high heat (400°F) until the skins start to turn black. Transfer them into a clean paper bag immediately, and leave them there until they're cool enough to handle. The condensation will soften the skins, making them easy to peel right off.

Phyllo Dough: An ingredient in sweet and savory Middle Eastern pastries, phyllo dough consists of paper-thin sheets that are coated with oil and baked until crispy. Some specialty stores sell phyllo dough in the refrigerator, rather than the freezer. If you can, buy yours at one of these stores; it'll be much easier to work with than if you buy it frozen. If you do buy it frozen, defrost it in the refrigerator for at least a day before you use it. Most recipes I've seen for dishes made with phyllo dough instruct you to cover it with a damp cloth while you're using it to keep it from drying out. I haven't found this to be necessary, but it may depend on the relative humidity of the climate where you live. If you find your phyllo dough drying out, cover it with a damp cloth while you work with it.

Pita Bread: In addition to the pita pockets we're all familiar with, pita sometimes comes in the form of a flatbread with no pocket. Known as "Greek pita," this flatbread is especially good if you heat it in a pan with just a bit of oil for about twenty seconds on each side. Dip the heated wedges in Hummus (page 2) or Baba Ghanoush (page 6), or serve them with Greek Salad (page 56). Use either kind of pita bread for Falafel (page 134).

Potatoes: Once considered a subsistence staple, these days potatoes are coming into their own as tasty, versatile vegetables, with countless varieties available. Russet potatoes are best for baking but shouldn't be used for other purposes. Smaller potatoes are the most special—and the most expensive. I like to mix red and white ones for maximum visual appeal. Many traditional cooks peel their potatoes, but the peels have plenty of flavor and also plenty of nutrients. Besides, why add an extra step to the cooking process?

Rice Flour: Made from uncooked rice ground to make flour, rice flour is a useful thickener for dishes cooked on the stovetop. It should be sprinkled into a dish toward the very end of the cooking process. I like it for thickening sauces and cooked fruit dishes because it is less likely to form lumps than wheat flour, and it thickens food immediately, unlike cornstarch, which you have to cook into foods in order to get them to thicken.

Rice Noodles: You can find many varieties of rice noodles in Asian markets. Those produced in China tend to be thin, like vermicelli. Those from Thailand are broader, coming in various widths, all of which are wider than Chinese rice noodles. The thinner noodles from China are less likely to stick together, so they're best for salads and other items meant to be eaten cold, like Spring Rolls (page 15). The broad noodles are best for Pad Thai (page 102).

Rice Vinegar: A relatively mild variety of vinegar made from rice wine, rice vinegar is used in many traditional Japanese dishes, especially sushi. You can get seasoned rice vinegar, which contains some sugar to balance its acidity, but for the recipes in this book you should buy "genuine brewed" rice vinegar.

Sea Salt: Unlike ordinary table salt, which is extracted from salt mines, sea salt is made by evaporating seawater. Sea salts from different parts of the world often have distinct flavors and colors, such as the grey Celtic kind and the pink Himalayan variety. Sea salt contains minerals not present in table salt, and these added nutrients also give it a deeper flavor.

Soy Sauce: A traditional, salty Japanese condiment made from fermented soybeans, soy sauce can be either an artisan product or a mass-produced grocery item. Quality soy sauce has a more complex flavor and fewer preservatives than the cheaper stuff, but if you check labels you can find inexpensive options that taste fine and have no chemicals. For a lower sodium, non-fermented alternative, you can substitute Bragg's Liquid Aminos for soy sauce in any recipe. It has no added salt, plenty of essential nutrients, and a wonderful flavor.

Squash: Winter squash comes in many varieties, from the dimpled acorn squash to the mighty pumpkin, which can weigh over a thousand pounds. Winter squash tends to be sweet and starchy, making it a great comfort food. You can bake it in the oven with some water in the pan to keep it moist, you can cut it into pieces that fit in your vegetable steamer, or you can peel it, cut it into bite-sized pieces, and sauté it with other vegetables. Whatever way you choose to cook it, make sure it's fork tender before you eat it.

Sugar: White table sugar is made from highly processed sugar cane or sugar beets. Its widespread use has been linked with epidemics of diabetes and obesity, although during the past few decades, as high-fructose corn syrup has become the sweetener of choice in cheap soft drinks, table sugar has come to be seen as somewhat more benign. Raw sugar, or granulated cane juice, is a somewhat less refined version of traditional white sugar. I like to use it for baking because it has a relatively clean taste, and its crystalline form makes it easy to use.

Tahini: A paste made of ground sesame seeds, tahini is used in many Middle Eastern dishes, especially dips. During the 1960s, pioneers of the natural foods movement embraced it as a healthful food, and began marketing their own brands. In my experience, tahini prepared and designed for a Middle Eastern market tastes better and blends more easily with other ingredients than tahini designed for a natural food market. Middle Eastern tahini is light and creamy, whereas the tahini usually sold in natural food stores often looks and tastes a lot like peanut butter. Sahadi and Joyva are my favorite widely available brands but, in general, if it has Arabic writing on the label or is made somewhere in the Middle East, it's a good bet.

Tamarind Paste: Made from a sweet-and-sour tropical fruit, tamarind paste is widely used in Indian and Southeast Asian dishes. You can find containers of tamarind paste in Asian and Indian groceries, and also in exemplary supermarkets.

Toasted Sesame Oil: An essential ingredient in Chinese and Korean cooking, toasted sesame oil has a deep, nutty flavor that helps give these cuisines their characteristic flavors. Sesame oil should be added to a dish toward the very end of the cooking process because it doesn't respond well to sustained, high heat. It's fairly perishable, so you should store it in the refrigerator or buy it in small bottles so it won't go rancid before you use it all.

Tofu: Also known as bean curd, tofu is a versatile, high-protein food commonly used in vegetarian cuisine. It doesn't have much taste of its own, but it is an excellent vehicle for other flavors, which it easily absorbs. Use soft tofu in recipes where it's pureed or crumbled, and firm or extra-firm tofu in recipes where it keeps its shape.

Tomatoes: Because there's such a dramatic difference between ripe, summer tomatoes and those rubbery specimens you find at the supermarket during the winter, it's best to save those salad recipes that include tomatoes for the hot, summer months. Because they're so juicy, overripe tomatoes work best in sauces, or any recipe where the tomatoes are cooked.

Umeboshi Plums and Umeboshi Paste: Umeboshi plums are a variety of salted Japanese plum that is often found in macrobiotic recipes. Umeboshi plums are highly alkaline, a property that can help to balance acidic conditions in the body, such as heartburn. Umeboshi paste is made from pureed umeboshi plums, and is great on nori rolls or incorporated into rice and tofu dishes.

Yams: These hearty tubers are commonly used in African and Caribbean cooking, and in foods from the southern United States. There are many different varieties grown all over the world, but the ones we most often see have a deep orange flesh and a sweet flavor. Yams are frequently confused with sweet potatoes, another variety of sweet tuber, but they are actually different species. With the exception of the Japanese Mountain yam, virtually all yams need to be cooked because they're toxic raw. You can roast them whole in the oven and then remove the flesh from the skins, or you can peel them with a good vegetable peeler, and them steam or sauté them.

Zucchini: A popular summer squash, zucchini is easy to prep and cooks quickly. It goes well with fresh herbs and other summer vegetables, such as tomatoes and peppers. Make sure not to overcook it, or it will lose its color and texture.

BASIC TECHNIQUES

COOKING BEANS, GRAINS, AND PASTA

Beans and grains are basic staples that make up an important part of a nutritious vegetarian or vegan diet. They can take extra time to prepare, so make sure to take this into account when you're planning your menu. Pasta is another important, versatile item to keep on hand.

BEANS

Soaking beans in water (about 1 inch deep over the beans) reduces their cooking time and saves energy, and also makes them more digestible. It's best to start soaking them the night before you use them, but if you don't remember or aren't planning that far ahead, a few hours, or even just an hour, will do. In a pinch, you can even cover the beans with water, bring them to a boil, and then change the water and start cooking them right away.

Always change the water you've used to soak the beans before you start cooking them, as the soaking water will have leached out some of the complex sugars and starches that can cause flatulence. Once you've added fresh, unsalted water and brought them to a boil, lower the heat and cook them on medium-low heat, uncovered, until they're soft. Keep an eye on them, stir them often, and add more water if the level starts to get low.

Smaller beans like red beans, white beans, and black beans take about an hour to cook, although they can take longer if they're old. Organic beans often take a little longer than those that are conventionally grown. Larger beans like chickpeas, or garbanzo beans, can take a couple of hours.

You can sometimes tell if beans are ready just by looking at them: the skins start to break when the insides are fully cooked. But you should always test them anyway, just to be sure. Try a couple of them, from different parts of the pot.

GRAINS

You can cook most grains in two parts of water to one part of grain. I cook rice, quinoa, barley, and millet this way. In fact, when I'm not sure how to cook a particular grain or even an unfamiliar variety of a familiar grain, I use these proportions and they almost always work. Wild rice requires three parts of water to one part of grain, and wheat berries and spelt berries use about 2 1/2 parts of water to 1 part of grain.

You can salt the water in which you're cooking your grain, or not. I tend not to. Alternatively, you can always cook grains in stock, or part stock and part water to give them a fuller flavor.

Bring the water to a boil before you add the grain. After you add the grain, bring the liquid back to a boil, cover the pot, and lower the heat to maintain a gentle simmer.

Barley, quinoa, and millet will cook in 15 or 20 minutes, while brown rice will take 30 to 45 minutes. Cook each of these grains until all of the water in the pot is absorbed. Don't stir them until you're ready to use them, as this makes them mushy and sticky. You can tell if your grain is ready by tilting the pot and seeing if there's any liquid left on the bottom.

PASTA

Aside from the well-known and beloved spaghetti, there are countless varieties of the semolina product known as pasta. Pasta is traditionally used in European foods, especially those with Mediterranean flavors, and also in Asian dishes from a variety of cultures.

In Western dishes the pastas that come in strands, like spaghetti and fettucini, work best with sauces like marinara and pesto. Other shapes, like spirals and the tubular ziti, penne, and rigatoni, are best in pasta salads or in dishes where the pasta is served with flavorful pieces, like olives and artichoke hearts.

I'm not a big fan of whole wheat pasta, although I know it has more nutri-ents than the white variety. I prefer a more delicate pasta, but if you feel differently you can use whole wheat pasta for any of the Mediterranean pasta recipes in this book. If you're allergic to wheat and you enjoy pasta, you should experiment with some of the gluten-free varieties available. They improve every year.

Asian dishes commonly use noodles that come in strands, such as the Chinese lo mein and the Japanese yakisoba. Many Asian cuisines also make use of pasta sheets to wrap savory fillings, as in the Chinese egg rolls and pot stickers. Asian recipes also use noodles made from rice, either the thin ones from China or the thicker ones from Thailand.

To prepare any kind of dried wheat pasta—Eastern or Western—boil about twice as much water as the pasta takes up in volume. You can add some vegetable oil to the water to keep the pasta from sticking together, but I don't think it's really necessary if you pay attention and stir it often while you're cooking it. Wait until the water is seriously boiling before you add the pasta, and always cook it uncovered. Most varieties of pasta are most prone to stick together during the first minute after you add them to the water. Stir them most attentively during that first minute, making sure that none of the pasta is sticking to the pan. After the first minute, you can stir it intermittently.

Cook pasta until it's soft all the way through, but not mushy. Take a piece out of the pot, wait a moment for it to cool, and then taste it to determine if it's soft enough. If it's ready, drain the pasta through a colander. Give it an extra moment to make sure all the water has drained, or else you'll end up diluting whatever tasty sauce you're mixing it with.

To cook the thin rice noodles from China, boil about twice as much water as the pasta takes up in volume. Turn off the flame, add the noodles, and let the noodles soak, uncovered, for about 10 minutes before draining them. You don't need to stir these. To cook the thicker rice noodles from Thailand, boil about twice as much water as the pasta takes up in volume, then turn off the heat, add the noodles, and let the noodles soak for two to three minutes, stirring them almost constantly so they don't stick together. Drain them well and use them as quickly as possible so they don't get sticky.

COOKING TECHNIQUES

Here are some basic cooking techniques that you'll find useful in preparing all kinds of vegan recipes.

FRYING

Immersing foods in oil to cook them is often called "deep-fat frying." This method creates the satisfying, chewy exterior that we're familiar with in so many of our comfort foods, like French fries and fried onion rings. Use a vegetable oil that can tolerate high heat, like peanut or corn oil. Never use olive oil for deep-frying. Heat about 1 inch of oil to about 360°F before you add the food you're frying. The temperature will drop as you add the food. Wait for it to increase again before adding more. If you don't have a thermometer, you can test to see if the oil is hot enough by tossing in a drop of water (but just one drop). If the oil is ready, the water will bounce off the surface.

Fry foods for a few minutes before turning them over and cooking them for a few minutes longer, until they're brown on both sides. Remove them from the oil with a slotted spoon, and drain them on paper towels or clean brown bags before serving.

GRILLING

Heating foods over an open flame is probably the most ancient cooking method of all. The high heat sears food on the outside, creating a tasty, crispy coating. These days we generally use a barbecue grill to keep food from sitting directly in the fire. Although grilling is a cooking technique most often used for meat, it also works well with vegetables.

You can cut your vegetables into pieces large enough that they won't fall through the slots on the grill, or your can use wooden skewers. I prefer skewers because they make portable, self-contained meals. If you're using skewers you should soak them in water for ten minutes or so before you use them so they don't catch on fire.

To grill vegetables, marinate them for at least 10 minutes. The longer you marinate them, the tastier they'll be, but it doesn't take long for them to start becoming flavorful. Any of the marinades in the Baked Tofu section of this book (pages 138–148) make great marinades for grilled vegetables as well.

If you're using skewers, arrange the marinated vegetables on the skewers and place them directly on the grill. Cook them for three or four minutes, then turn them over so they're attractively browned on both sides.

ROASTING

This is the process of cooking in the oven on high heat (at least 400°F), concentrating flavors and caramelizing foods by drawing out their sugars. To roast vegetables, cut them into bite-sized pieces. If you're using root vegetables it's a good idea to parboil them by boiling them in water for a minute or two before you roast them. To roast the vegetables, toss them with enough oil to coat them and a little bit of salt (about $1/2$ teaspoon per pound of veggies). You can also include any kind of dried or fresh herb that you like. Spread the coated pieces in a thin layer on a baking sheet and cook them until they start to brown. This usually takes about 30 or 40 minutes. For roasting nuts, see Pantry, page 211.

SAUTÉING

This is the process of cooking food in enough oil to coat it, while stirring it often. I usually sauté vegetables on a medium-low flame, but that can vary depending on how many items I've got on the stovetop at once. I'll use a higher flame if I'm giving a dish my undivided attention, and a lower one if I'm not attending to it as fully.

In most recipes you should sauté onions and garlic first (along with shallots, leeks, and/or ginger, if you're using them). Cook these ingredients until the onions (and shallots) are translucent, and until the garlic is aromatic. Add the other vegetables in order from the hardest to the softest, with the exception of eggplant, which should be added early because it takes a while to cook.

It's important to use enough oil to coat the onions and garlic because the oil helps them reach a temperature hot enough for them to release their flavors, but you can use other liquids, such as soy sauce, to keep the other vegetables from sticking to the pan once the onions and garlic are fully cooked.

STEAMING

This is the process of cooking vegetables over (but not directly in) boiling water. This technique cooks veggies quickly while preserving many of their nutrients. If you don't have a pot specifically designed for steaming, most supermarkets carry inexpensive steamer baskets that fit in a wide range of small- to medium-sized pots. Always cover the pan when you're steaming vegetables. In a pinch, you can arrange a colander over an inch or so of boiling water in a pan, and cover it as tightly as you can with whatever lid you have available.

Most veggies cut into bite-sized pieces will be fully cooked once you steam them for about three minutes, although some harder veggies, like carrots and potatoes, take a bit longer and some greens, such as spinach, only take a minute. Don't steam veggies to the point where they lose their color. Check them often and get to know your personal preferences for how fully you like particular veggies to be cooked.

INDEX